# LONDON
## IN THE
# WILD

**An Hachette UK Company**
www.hachette.co.uk

First published in Great Britain in 2022 by
**Kyle Books**, an imprint of Octopus
Publishing Group Limited
Carmelite House
50 Victoria Embankment
London EC4Y 0DZ
**www.kylebooks.co.uk**

ISBN: 9780857839947

*Publishing Director* **Judith Hannam**
*Publisher* **Joanna Copestick**
*Design* **Helen Bratby**
*Cover illustration* **Jane Newland**
*Editor* **Jenny Dye**
*Production* **Caroline Alberti**

A Cataloguing in Publication record for this title is
available from the British Library

Printed and bound in China

10 9 8 7 6 5 4 3 2 1

# LONDON
## IN THE
# WILD

EXPLORING NATURE IN THE CITY

KYLE BOOKS

TOP ROW: BEAULIEU HEIGHTS; SPECKLED WOOD BUTTERFLY; REEDBED MANAGEMENT 2ND ROW: CYCLISTS AT ONE TREE HILL; SYDENHAM HILL WOOD; KEEPING IT WILD TRAINEES. 3RD ROW: PEREGRINE FALCON; WOODBERRY WETLANDS, HARBOUR SEAL; BOTTOM ROW: SOUTHWELL ROAD; CHARLIE, A TRAINEE; WELSH HARP (BRENT) RESERVOIR

# CONTENTS

06   Foreword by Chris Packham

08   Introduction

10   The River Thames: London's largest open space

24   Wild nightlife & urban wildlife

42   Created spaces: ecology parks, nature reserves, city farms & community gardens

78   The glory of parks: where nature rules

96   London's heathlands: a unique landscape

108   Autumn in London's woodlands

120   Wetlands & reservoirs: a visit on a winter's morning

136   London's grasslands: a summer's day in a meadow

158   Top 10 hidden gems

180   The future of conservation: a young Londoner's view

182   How-to guides

186   Contributors

188   Index

190   References & resources

191   Picture credits

192   Acknowledgements

# CHRIS PACKHAM

It's easy to think that 'London' and 'nature' don't go together. We often think of London as a place of noise and pollution, a harsh urban environment that's been created for people and has pushed wildlife away.

In previous years we rushed through the city, focused on our destination, wrapped up in our thoughts. But in 2020 life took a strange turn and London became unusually silent and still. With many aspects of life curtailed, lots of us started to spend more time in our local areas, with daily walks in our parks and commons becoming our main pastime.

Many Londoners discovered their local nature and green spaces and found that the city's seemingly urban sprawl is teeming with wildlife ready to be discovered and enjoyed.

*London in the Wild* is a timely opportunity to get out and explore all the wild spaces and natural places that exist alongside you – both on your doorstep and on the other side of the river.

In 2020 London's nature and wildlife provided solace and peace for so many at a time when we desperately needed it. We must not forget that nature needs our support, too. Wild spaces in urban environments are as uniquely vulnerable as they are precious. Many people and organisations, including London Wildlife Trust, have been working behind the scenes for years to make sure that the parks and green spaces we've all been enjoying are protected and can flourish in the future.

I invite you to explore and discover nature in our city and I hope that you feel inspired to protect London's nature for the future.

# INTRODUCTION

BY MATHEW FRITH, DIRECTOR OF RESEARCH AND POLICY AT LONDON WILDLIFE TRUST

In May 1981 London Wildlife Trust's founders set out the Primrose Hill Declaration, a manifesto and clarion call to gain support for their work. It set out a vision for a greener, more environmentally sensitive and more inclusive London.

Rooted in the actions taken by people in Victorian times to protect some of London's great landscapes from being built on, and prevent wildlife being persecuted, it placed the embryonic Trust in that framework – a collectivist, grassroots approach to putting nature back in the heart of the city. Its language may have become dated since then, but the overall objectives that the Declaration calls for are as relevant today as ever.

*We are all trustees of London's heritage. We recognise that what has already been achieved in conserving and enhancing the environment has been by dint of local group and community effort and organisation. We are aware that these initiatives have followed from the well springs of social concern that established the fundamental right to clean air, pure water and good housing. To these, we can now add the right to share our environment with nature and wildlife.*

*A century ago London people pioneered the use of common land for public amenity at Epping Forest and Wimbledon common: now is the time for conservationists to take up the common ground throughout London. In the inner city and around the suburbs, our natural heritage is still enclosed within corrugated iron, despoiled or locked behind chain-link fencing. This has been the expropriation of London's natural heritage by industry, development, greed, waste and misconception.*

*Conservation will liberate this heritage for everyone to enjoy. Through a renaissance of care for environment, London's countryside can be recovered; nature and wildlife will reclaim yet the smallest open space on street or window ledges.*

**WE, THE LONDON WILDLIFE TRUST, THEREFORE AFFIRM THE RIGHTS OF LONDON'S PEOPLE TO:**

- *clean air*
- *unpolluted water*
- *the integrity of our ecological world for our children and theirs*
- *ample open space as in the best of the countryside*
- *live and plan in harmony with wildlife*
- *determine the reasonable use of our land and resources*

Today the Trust is a driving force for nature conservation. We strive to protect London's wildlife and enhance the habitats on which it depends. We take action every day to help it flourish through practical conservation; we engage, inspire and enable people to connect with nature, and through campaigns, collaboration and advice we help give wildlife a stake in London. We can't do this without our members, volunteers, supporters and partners, who help us to make sure London is wilder, now and for the future.

*London in the Wild* gives an overview of the diversity of wild animals, plants and fungi found in the city. It draws on the expertise of many voices, some of whom work for us, and others who work alongside us; all dedicate their time to London's nature and we value their collective insight. Readers will discover more about some of London's most important habitats from the River Thames to ancient forests and chalk grasslands. There are descriptions of hidden corners, some history and thoughts for the future, as well as tips to help wildlife. The book doesn't pretend to cover all of the species and wild places of London; we aim to present a flavour of London's wild, and exhibit the passion of those working to champion it. As such some of the sites and wildlife featured reflect the choices of the contributors (see pages 186–7).

If you're new to discovering wildlife in London you'll quickly find that nature can surprise us, but you do need to get your eye in; 'look up' for birds and trees, 'look down' for street flowers, beetles and bugs. Little of the city is rolling green countryside, but there's always something special about nature finding a foot amongst the bricks and mortar. We hope that this book helps readers to discover the nature on their doorsteps. In turn, we look forward to a new generation joining us to protect nature's place in the city, and make London's future a place where the amazing diversity of wildlife we share our city with is rightly cherished.

## NOTES

# THE RIVER THAMES

# LONDON'S LARGEST OPEN SPACE

The River Thames is the UK's most iconic river. The tidal portion flows 153km (95 miles) from Teddington, west London, and joins the North Sea at an invisible boundary running between Shoeburyness, in Essex, and Sheerness, in Kent. Known as the Port of London, the tidal Thames was once the largest port in the world and today is still one of the UK's biggest. Our local patch of the global ocean, the Thames, built the city of London we know today through access to international trade.

The tidal River Thames is London's largest open space, a playground for walkers, water sports enthusiasts and tourists. Some of the UK's most important heritage destinations are found on its banks, along with tranquil spots offering astonishing peace and quiet. Although millions of people visit the Thames every year to see the sights and experience the river, most don't realise that the Thames is a wildlife superhighway. With **125 species of fish**, as well as **shellfish**, **seals**, **dolphins**, **porpoises** and **birds**, it is one of the UK's most biodiverse places, attracting both resident wildlife and visiting wildlife migrating from one part of the ocean to another.

What lies unseen beneath the water remains a mystery to many. Here we will bring this underwater wonderland to life with tales of the unexpected, weird and wonderful creatures you can see almost every day if you just know where to look.

# THE TIDAL THAMES

A bird's eye view of Greater London and the surrounding areas would reveal that the land forms a very large bowl, with London and the Thames at the bottom of it. This is known as a river basin, and all the water flowing down each of the rivers of London, including the Thames above Teddington, flows into the tidal Thames at the bottom, and this flows on into the global ocean. It is one huge, interconnected system circulating fresh and marine water that supports a wealth of wildlife throughout.

The tidal Thames is an estuary, which essentially is the sea reaching up into the landscape twice a day on a tidal cycle. Like the tide on a beach, it has a high tide and a low tide each day and is subject to monthly cycles where the tidal range grows and shrinks. These very high and very low tides (in other words, those with the greatest range) are known as spring tides, while very small high and low tides (with the smallest range) are called neap tides.

As the tide flows in and ebbs out, it lifts the sediment off the riverbed and mixes it in the water, giving the river its signature brown colour. This is often misunderstood as a sign that it is dirty, but that couldn't be further from the truth. The mixing of sediment and water releases nutrients and tiny animals such as zooplankton and invertebrates into the water, making the river an extremely nutritious feeding ground. Its murkiness provides excellent cover for fish hiding from predators in the air and underwater, and the tidal energy allows fish and marine mammals to ride the tide, surfing up and down as needed.

What you will find where depends on the daily tidal cycle, the speed of the water flow, how much salt is in the water and the availability of access to areas where wildlife can shelter, feed and breed. These factors vary according to season and rainfall, but there are characteristic wildlife found throughout the tidal Thames and some that are only found in specific areas. Let's start at the top of the tidal Thames, at Teddington, and follow the tide out to the ocean.

# Teddington to Putney

The upper reaches of the tidal Thames, from Teddington to Putney, are almost entirely freshwater with just a very small amount of salt from the sea. The water from the upstream Thames and rivers flows into the estuary, mixing with the seawater flowing in on the tide.

The plant and animal species within this stretch of the river are a reflection of the various habitats and the dominance of freshwater. Here, the river is a leafy, open stretch meandering through a landscape lined with wet woodlands. Islets are dotted throughout (aits and eyots – Old English for 'small islands'). The riverside, including the Thames Path, is designed to flood on a high tide, with sections of the floodplain reconnected to the river through inlets and back channels. The largest stretch of natural riverbank within the tidal Thames between Teddington and Dartford is at Syon Park. There are plenty of places along the river where wildlife can feed and shelter. Freshwater shrimps and snails provide a valuable food source for fish such as dace and roach, barbel, bream, carp and pike, and for summer visitors migrating upstream such as flounder, smelt and goby. The gravelly foreshore is perfect for freshwater mussels and is an important habitat for common smelt (a fish) to lay their eggs. Overhanging vegetation, backwaters and islands provide nesting and roosting sites for kingfisher, great crested grebe, moorhen, coot, mallard and heron. In the winter this stretch is important for tufted duck and teal. The leafy riverside is also a feeding ground for bats.

# Chelsea to Gravesend

In the vicinity of Chelsea, the Thames starts to change, with the sloping riverbanks giving way to vertical river walls colonised by red and green algae. This section of the tidal Thames is placed under considerable stress from both the rise and fall of the tide and the changing proportions of fresh and saltwater. Along this stretch the water gets increasingly salty as it gets closer to the ocean. This is the most urban and industrial part of the river – the water flows very fast and there is little habitat at the edges for wildlife to rest or feed. Not much stays here, because of the turbulent water and slippery vertical walls. Instead, it can be imagined as the motorway of the Thames, with wildlife passing through en route from one end to the other.

To mimic nature, terraces, known as Estuary Edges, have been built into the river walls, creating stepping stones of habitat for wildlife. Examples can be found at the top of this middle section at Wandsworth Riverside Quarter and at Battersea Reach. They don't occur again until the Greenwich Peninsula Terraces North East and North West (see page 50), mainly because there is no space available for building such sites through the central section.

The river starts to widen out below Tower Bridge, and old redundant structures such as disused jetties and piers dot the river edges. These structures play an important role in providing high tide resting places and nest sites for birds such as common tern.

From around Deptford, tidal creeks and tidal sections of rivers such as the Lea, Barking Creek and Darent play an increasingly important role for fish. They have more areas of habitat, such as reedbeds at the river edges, and are excellent areas to shelter and feed. Estuary Edges sites also begin to become more frequent and provide shelter for baby fish on a flooding tide. These vegetated terraces are also good foraging sites for bees and land mammals such as bank voles. From around Erith onwards, the riverside habitat starts to become more natural, with areas of saltmarsh and grazing marsh, and the foreshore becomes predominantly muddy, which is perfect for marine worms – the main food source for overwintering wildfowl and waders.

# Gravesend to the North Sea

From Gravesend downstream to the tidal end at the North Sea, the river becomes fully marine, in terms of both salt content and riverside habitats, and looks much more like a coastal environment. The river channel gets ever wider, and habitats along the edges include saltmarsh, reedbeds and mudflats, shell and shingle banks and saline lagoons. Saltmarsh and the large expanses of intertidal and subtidal mud provide rich feeding grounds for birds such as oystercatcher, dunlin, shelduck, teal and wigeon. The saltmarshes are important breeding and nursery grounds for fish such as Dover sole, flounder, sea bass and mullet feeding the commercial fish stocks of the North Sea. Many other species of fish can be found in this stretch, including flounder, goby, herring, plaice, pouting, sea lamprey, shad, smelt, sole, sprat, trout and whiting. The intertidal areas (which are covered at high tide and uncovered at low tide) and subtidal areas (which are shallow but always underwater) are also rich shellfish grounds, with cockles, whelks and oysters providing an important commercial fishery and bird feeding ground.

The river's body of water itself is home to moon jellyfish and comb jellyfish, planktons, such as diatoms, copepods and amphipods. Invertebrates found here include brown shrimp and opossum shrimp, prawns, marine worms and shore crabs.

# THE RIVER'S MIGRATORY ANIMALS

There are a few animals that need both freshwater and marine conditions at different stages of their lives, and they need to move from one end of the river to the other. Additionally, there are species that can tolerate the changing conditions and will move around in the river, feeding and exploring.

Marine mammals such as seals, dolphins and porpoises are perhaps the most exciting to spot in the river. We have two types of seal in the Thames – the common or harbour seal and the grey seal – and they can be spotted anywhere in the tidal Thames. The two species can be distinguished by size (harbour seals are smaller than grey seals), shape of head (harbour seals have a stout nose, while grey seals have a longer nose) and 'haul-out' behaviour (harbour seals tend to spread out after leaving the water, whereas grey seals remain in close groups near the water).

The mudflats, sandflats and intertidal sandbanks in the estuary are their favourite spots to haul out of the water to rest, breed and moult. You can often see them sunning themselves in these areas of the marine Thames, but if you're lucky you may spot one on a patch of foreshore in central London, hauled out on a floating mooring or catching a fish in the river even further upstream.

We have permanent seal populations that breed in the marine stretches of the Thames Estuary and Greater Thames Estuary (the coast and low-lying lands bordering the Thames Estuary) and transient groups that travel between the Thames and The Wash (a sizeable estuary on England's east coast). Seal population surveys carried out in 2017 by the Zoological Society of London (ZSL) recorded 1,104 harbour seals and 2,406 grey seals across the Thames Estuary.

# Harbour seals

Harbour seals love to eat a wide variety of fish, such as herring, sand eel, whiting and flatfish, as well as shrimps and squid. They are frequently spotted foraging for food right through London all the way upstream to Teddington.

They mate in the summer and give birth, or 'pup', about 42 weeks later. Only one pup is born and is so well developed that it is able to swim and dive within just a few hours of birth. This means they can breed in the estuary where sandbanks are exposed for only part of the day, on the low tide. In 2018, ZSL conducted the first-ever count of seal pups born in the estuary. The results showed that 138 pups had arrived in one season.

After the pupping season ends, adults begin their annual 'moult', meaning they shed their fur. This usually lasts from mid-summer until September and they need to spend longer periods hauled out ashore. This is because as they lose their fur, they start to circulate blood to the surface of their skin to encourage replacement growth. The process requires a lot of energy, which means they need to keep warm and dry in the sun and avoid prolonged cooling in the water. They also tend to haul out after feeding to rest, much like we do after a good roast meal.

During the winter, harbour seals spend less time on shore and in the Thames, and more time out in the North Sea.

# Grey seals

Grey seals like the same types of fish as harbour seals but are also known to eat harbour seal pups and harbour porpoises. They mate in the winter, and, similarly to harbour seals, females give birth to a single pup about 11 months later (between November and January). Survey data suggests that, unlike the harbour seals, grey seals don't breed in the Thames Estuary – instead they are seasonal visitors. They tend to disperse further north along the English east coast as far as The Wash, or to mainland Europe during the breeding season.

Grey seals also haul out, usually twice a year: during the pupping season and then later during the spring, when they gather in large groups. Young grey seals usually moult first, followed by adult females, and finally by adult males. Once the moult is complete, they all head out to sea until the following winter.

Grey seal numbers have rapidly increased over the last 15 years, especially along the east coast of England, probably because they are no longer hunted by people for their fur. The increased numbers suggest that the number of grey seals using the outer Thames Estuary in summer months may be growing.

Seals are known to have similar intelligence levels to dogs and are very curious creatures. They like to investigate the world around them and will often approach boats, kayaks and paddleboards to find out what they are. Londoners who use the river regularly will often report that a friendly seal climbed onto their paddleboard or kayak for a rest in the Upper Thames.

Just as with any wild animal, they are wary of people and although seals are friendly, they are extremely strong and can be ferocious if feeling threatened. If you see them hauled out, never approach them – just enjoy watching them from afar. If you're walking along the beach, don't walk between them and the water, as this is their escape route. If they decide you are a predator, they will quickly tell you to leave and can charge at you. They may look clumsy on land but can move very fast!

# Other marine mammals

Harbour porpoise are the smallest whales in Europe, measuring 1.4–1.9m (4ft 6in–6ft 3in) in length. They are part of the family of 'toothed whales' that includes dolphins, killer whales and sperm whales. Due to their small size, harbour porpoises have to feed almost continuously on many small fish species and occasionally squid. They are very shy animals and won't be seen in the river near central London because of the noise and boat traffic. Their small dorsal fin and lack of jumping or splashing activity makes them very hard to spot in the river, which is partly why there is little known about their life in the Thames.

Dolphins have been recorded as far upriver as Tower Bridge but are a very rare sight in London.

# Fish migration

Many fish species undertake migrations on time scales ranging from daily to yearly and across distances spanning from a few metres to thousands of kilometres. Most migrations are for feeding or breeding purposes, but for some fish the reason for migration is unknown.

Fish species that migrate between salt and freshwater environments are referred to as diadromous fish, which are either anadromous and catadromous.

Anadromous fish are born in freshwater and then migrate to the ocean, where they mature into adults before returning to freshwater habitats to spawn. Species include salmon, smelt, shad, bass, lamprey and sturgeon.

Catadromous fish are born in the ocean and migrate into freshwater habitats, then eventually return to the ocean to spawn. The best-known is the European eel.

# European eel

This mighty migrator is London's most iconic fish, once caught frequently and sold as jellied eel and eel pie and mash. The European eel can still be found in a variety of freshwater and estuarine habitats. However, since the 1980s, adult populations have declined dramatically and the European eel is now classified as Critically Endangered by the IUCN (International Union for Conservation of Nature). One of the reasons is the barriers placed in rivers for water management, such as sluices and weirs, that stop eels from migrating and reaching their preferred habitat.

The European eel has one of the most fascinating life histories of any animal, though much of it remains a mystery, as tracking them over long distances is a technical challenge. The European eel's life cycle is thought to begin in the Sargasso Sea (in the North Atlantic Ocean), where it is born in larval form – small, translucent leaf-like creatures called leptocephali. From there, they float on ocean currents until they reach European rivers, including the River Thames and its tributaries.

Once here, they start the metamorphosis that is triggered by nearing a river mouth. First they transform into the colourless miniature eels known as glass eels, when they reach the continental shelf; then when they arrive at the estuary, they transform into elvers, pigmenting into a muddy brown colour which camouflages them in the silty water. Once in the estuary, they will follow their noses, searching for freshwater. Eels can detect minuscule amounts of freshwater using receptors in their snouts, and they will keep swimming until they find a freshwater river they like. During this time they will grow into yellow eels – brown on the top and yellow on the underside, to reflect their freshwater surroundings so they can hide from predators. Here they will stay while they get bigger and fatter, transforming into a full adult silver eel.

At some point up to 20 years later, they will make one last transformation in preparation for the long transatlantic journey back to the Sargasso Sea. Their eyes grow very large and their snouts elongate ready for swimming through the ocean, answering the call to return and mate. From the point at which they leave to return to the ocean, they do not stop to eat. They will swim until they reach their spawning grounds, where they mate and then die, becoming a nutritious meal for some lucky ocean animals. Eels favour the river bottom at the edges, where it's dark and easy to hide. For this reason they can often be found in sewage pipes and water management structures. They are resourceful migrators, able to climb walls and cross wet meadows as long as there is enough roughness for them to get traction for moving along. Sometimes an elver will remain in the estuary for a year or two, hiding under rocks on the foreshore at low tide.

If you take a walk on the foreshore, trying lifting a rock here and there to see if you can spot one waiting for the tide to come back in. Eels do not like to be handled, though, so if you do want to pick it up, wet your hands first, be gentle and be prepared for some sticky mucous exuding from its body. This is a defence mechanism to predators but it won't hurt you.

Be careful picking anything up from the foreshore or the water, and always wash your hands before handling food, eating or drinking, as there are human and animal bacteria and viruses in the water that could make you sick. The Thames foreshore is not a maintained environment – it is essentially a wild space. It can be very uneven underfoot, so always wear sturdy footwear. Check the tide times and make sure you know where your next exit is to get back onto the Thames Path, to avoid getting caught out by the incoming tide.

# German hairy snail: ancient grazer of Thames litter

In 1957 the River Thames was declared biologically dead; it had been pretty much dead since the 'Great Stink' of 1858, which had forced Parliament to decamp temporarily to Oxford. From the 1960s, successive efforts to reduce industrial pollution, remove debris and prevent untreated sewage entering the Thames have made it significantly cleaner. Now the 125 species of fish found within its waters range from salmon to seahorses, and these in turn have supported the return of birds such as common tern, grey heron, cormorant and shelduck.

The Thames is a complex, constantly changing river, and within London we see it ebb and flow twice daily, freshwaters flowing downstream from the west mixing with salty tides from the east. As such it remains forever brown as it churns the silt and sand it holds within its writhing channel, and also collects the litter that still finds its way into its grasp. Much of this is plastic and wood, either bobbing in the waves or stranded on the banks as the tides subside.

Much of this litter winds up held within bankside vegetation and around a stretch of the river between Barnes Bridge and Isleworth, affording a peculiar home for

two small molluscs: the two-lipped door snail, *Balea biplicata*, and the German hairy snail, *Pseudotrichia rubiginosa*. Both are rare in Britain, now occurring principally at sites along the tidal Thames, such as Isleworth Ait and Lot's Ait (islets in the river, at Isleworth and Brentford respectively), Duke's Hollow in Chiswick, but also in the Lower Lea Valley near Bow.

A primarily eastern European mollusc, first formally recognised in Britain in 1982 at Syon Marsh (now part of Syon Park in Isleworth), the German hairy snail is assigned the status Vulnerable in the British Red Data Books (an inventory of animals and plants at risk of extinction). It has a flattened, reddish-brown, convex-whorled shell, about 4–9mm (a scant ¼–⅜in) in diameter, characteristically covered on the upper surface with tiny hairlike spikes (periostracal hairs) although when the shell ages, these hairs, which are thought to help it adhere to the dead vegetation it feeds on, are often absent.

The snail is a grazer, using its rasping file-like mouth ('radula') to remove dead and decaying plant material and diatoms (tiny, single-cell plants) that coat the surfaces of roots, stones and other material. It typically lives among flood debris and dead leaves in muddy, poorly vegetated ground, sometimes shaded by willow trees. However, surveys over the past 20 years have shown that the largest concentrations of snails have been found under planks, plastic sacks and general rubbish. It appears that these have become preferred habitats for the snail.

Surprisingly, a shell of the species was retrieved from late Bronze Age archaeological excavations in Runnymede in 1987; it was estimated to date from c.830 BC. The German hairy snail is now thought to have arrived in Britain during the last Ice Age when Britain and mainland Europe were conjoined. It seems highly likely that this tiny mollusc has been present in the Thames Valley at least since that time, but has always remained rare and largely invisible until plastic litter became common from the 1970s onwards. After all, it is a tiny snail, not easily seen unless looked for.

Progress in enhancing the ecological quality of the Thames continues, and actions to remove plastic litter from the river have justifiably strong political and public support. However, these are appearing to inadvertently contribute to a decline in the German hairy snail's abundance and distribution in recent years, which is

echoed by that of the two-lipped door snail, which appears to have become extinct from Isleworth Ait, despite its nocturnal behaviour of climbing trees. Whether such adaptable snails can be encouraged to return to a more natural habitat remains to be seen, but their rarity from a British perspective helps to focus conservation efforts on where they live; indeed, a highlight for the Mayor of Hounslow was when she briefly held a German hairy snail on her visit to Isleworth Ait in 2014.

## NOTES

Chapter 2 BY MATHEW FRITH

# WILD NIGHTLIFE & URBAN WILDLIFE

# LONDON'S WILD NIGHTLIFE

It's a quiet night right on the edges of London. Apart from the tarmac roar of the distant A40, only the languid ripples of a river and the whispering swish of mature alders and willows break the silence under an almost cloudless, ultramarine sky. There are six of us, well wrapped even though it's June, slowly ambling up a wooded track and hoping to witness a rare sight in the capital. Then, almost out of nowhere, a soft greenish fluorescence – like a tiny cat's-eye – shimmers into view. This is bioluminescence in action; that of a glow-worm trying to attract mates in the gloom. Glow-worms are beetles, and the light emits from the larviform females' abdomens by oxidation of a chemical with the devilish name of luciferin.

Over in the Lower Lea Valley, some 15km (9 miles) away, another group of nocturnal wanderers are searching by a reservoir against an orange sky. They have small boxes, mostly held aloft, and a couple carry torches or smartphones on full beam to help them navigate. Every so often the boxes stutter out a crescendo of clatter-clicks, causing hushed whoops of delight. They are picking up the sonar calls of bats, usually pipistrelles but also noctule, Daubenton's and Leisler's bats, as they seek moths and midges over the water's edge.

Whether it's the light pulses of glow-worms or the pippity-clicks of bats, most of this nightlife goes unnoticed. Humans have evolved to be active during daylight, with good daytime vision but pretty limited senses of hearing and smell. So it takes effort by intrepid naturalists to get a picture of how most nocturnal animals behave, how they navigate an increasingly lit London, and how best we design and manage our city to give them the room to flourish.

# LIVELY NIGHT-TIMES

London is rapidly becoming a 24/7 city. With several Tube lines having opened as all-hour services on Fridays and Saturdays, gradually the city's night has changed – and with it our impact on the capital's wildlife. What are the implications for the wildlife which have different nocturnal rhythms and needs to us?

More than 15,000 species of fungi, plants and animals, most of them wild, have been recorded in London. A significant number of these are crepuscular (active at dusk) or nocturnal. Most mammals are active during the night, including the eight species of bat recorded in London, as well as shrews, mole, hedgehog, bank vole, wood mouse, stoat, badgers, fox and the four species of deer, which is why they remain elusive, apart from their mating calls or, in the case of the fox and badger, the disruption they sometimes cause to litter bins or gardens.

Deer, while commonly seen in herds during the day, use darkness to break cover and feed. The muntjac, a small dog-sized deer native to China, which escaped from Bedfordshire's Woburn Park in about 1925 and is now widespread in many of London's outer boroughs, has a characteristic call that gives it its other name – the barking deer. One herd of fallow deer has become bolder, regularly wandering around an estate in east London, almost oblivious to the cars and night buses;

the animals can be seen silhouetted against the warm yellowing streetlight glow.

Amphibians are nocturnal, as are a number of fish, especially European eel and stone loach. Some key groups of invertebrates are also active at night, notably moths but also lacewings, ground beetles, rove beetles (including glow-worm), silverfish, spiders, centipedes, earthworms and many molluscs. While the four owls residing in London – tawny, barn, little and short-eared – are associated with nocturnal habits, they're not the only birds active in town overnight; blackbird, song thrush, robin, blackcap, snipe and woodcock are just a few of the birds that don't necessarily shut their eyes at sunset.

Nightingales may never have sung in Berkeley Square, but in Twickenham, along the River Crane, you may hear the marsh frog, a species introduced to the country in the 1920s on Romney Marsh. Their nocturnal calls can be surprisingly loud, if not mellifluous (they're more of a rasping burble), especially in early spring, and have led to their being known as marsh nightingales.

We don't know exactly how nocturnal species are responding to London (and the changes to its night-times) as so many are under-recorded. It's only comparatively recently – with the development of bat box

# ALL DAY
# & ALL NIGHT?

technologies – that we're beginning to get an insight into the behaviour of bats in London. For many other species, our information is based on anecdotal evidence or research conducted in cities elsewhere in the world.

A recent report suggests that there are now fewer than a million hedgehogs left in Britain, down from 36 million in the 1950s and an estimated 2 million in the mid-1990s. An insectivore that for much of the 20th century was associated with London parks, gardens and woodlands, the hedgehog has become increasingly scarce, particularly in our capital. A small population in Regent's Park may be the only colony left in central London; elsewhere, hedgehogs are increasingly only found in the outer suburbs (although comprehensive data is lacking) – see pages 76 and 77. What we've done to our gardens and the poisoning of hedgehog prey (through pesticides) are undoubtedly influential, but so too are our roads and the growth of late-night traffic.

It is likely that an ill-planned but vibrant night-time economy, with its attendant lighting, increased traffic, noise and firework displays, could lead to ruin for much of our nocturnal wildlife. As we learn more about how these species use London between dusk and dawn, we should put in place measures that minimise harmful impacts and give space to them under dark skies.

Many years ago I was asked to cut down a line of trees because of the birds that sang in them. I used to be responsible for the trees and green spaces of a social housing landlord, working to ensure that these were maintained and improved for the benefit of our residents. As always, talking with the residents revealed very different views, in this case a line of cherry trees where my plan for a judicious prune wasn't enough. 'Can you fell all them trees, please? The birds keep us awake all night because of their bloody singing...' Here was a sign that nature disrupts our night-time habits and that our nocturnal behaviour is increasingly disrupting nature.

London's night-time has become brighter; even by 2003 the sky above London was described as 91 per cent light-saturated. Transport corridors have long been sources of light pollution, but sports grounds, illuminated advertising and security lighting are increasingly affecting nocturnal wildlife.

Artificial light disrupts natural patterns of light and dark, disturbing invertebrate feeding, breeding and movement. Some invertebrates, such as moths, are attracted to artificial lights at night. As many as a third of flying insects attracted to external lights will die as a result of their encounter; insects can become disoriented and exhausted, making them more susceptible to predation. In addition, the polarisation of light by shiny surfaces attracts insects, particularly egg-laying females,

away from water. Reflected light can attract pollinators, impacting on their populations, predators and pollination rates. Many invertebrates' natural rhythms depend upon day–night, seasonal and lunar changes, which can be adversely affected by artificial lighting.

British bat species have all suffered dramatic reductions in their numbers over the past century, and for this reason they are now afforded legal protection from disturbance. Light falling on a bat roost exit point will delay bats from emerging, which shortens the amount of time available to them for foraging. Because the main peak of nocturnal insect abundance occurs at and soon after dusk, a delay in emergence means this vital time for feeding is missed. At worst, the bats may feel compelled to abandon the roost where they shelter and breed. Bats are faithful to their roosts over many years and disturbance of this sort can have a significant effect on the future of a colony. There is also a good case that excessive lighting can breach legislation that protects British bats and their roosts.

In addition to disturbing bats at the roost, artificial lighting influences the feeding behaviour of bats and their use of foraging routes along which they hunt. But it's not a simple picture; some species are attracted to lights because they attract their prey, while others avoid it. Many night-flying species of insect, such as moths, midges and lacewings, are attracted to lamps that emit short-wavelength light. Studies have shown that, although noctule, serotine, pipistrelle and Leisler's bats take advantage of insects around white street lights as a source of prey, this behaviour is not true for all bats. The slower-flying, broad-winged species, such as long-eared, Daubenton's and natterer's bats, generally avoid external lights.

The spectra of light used – as well as the move from sodium and halogen lighting to light-emitting diodes (LEDs) – are as influential as the brightness and location. A recent German study has shown that the replacement of conventional bulbs in street lighting by energy-saving LEDs has considerable influence on bats' urban nocturnal hunting. Opportunistic bats – such as those adapted to hunting light-attracted insect prey – lose hunting opportunities, whereas light-sensitive species benefit. Lighting can also be particularly harmful if it illuminates important foraging habitats used by bats, such as river corridors, field hedgerows and woodland edges. Studies have also shown that continuous lighting along roads creates barriers that some bat species will not cross.

# SMARTER LIGHTING, DARKER SKIES?

Birds, too, are affected by light; all are governed by the 24-hour cycle – the circadian rhythm – of day and night. The onset of the dawn chorus is triggered by a combination of the birds' internal clocks and the very first rays of sunlight. Even low light intensities can trigger song in some birds, and because they continue singing until dusk, the singing period can easily be extended into the night if lighting is of sufficient intensity.

The robin is the most common night-time songster in London. Research suggests that city lights convince many birds that there is no end to the day. Robins are adapted to hunting insects in dim light, so may be particularly sensitive to artificial light; blue light from neon signs is especially disruptive to a bird's circadian rhythm. However, the reasons for the robins' nocturnal singing have been a subject of some debate. Another view is that the birds predominantly sing at night in urban areas because it is too noisy during the day, so they have adapted to attract their mates and defend their territories with more crepuscular choruses. While singing through the night takes up a lot of energy, research has shown that it does not appear to have a significant effect on the birds' body-mass regulation. However, the continual lack of sleep is likely to be detrimental to their survival and could disrupt the long-term circadian rhythm that dictates the onset of the breeding season.

Many species of bird migrate at night. During autumn, flocks of thrushes – redwing and fieldfare – migrate from Iceland and Scandinavia at night, navigating by the stars; on a quiet night you might hear the soft, high-pitched 'seep-seep' contact calls of redwings. But birds can easily be disorientated by lights. There are well-documented cases of the mass mortality of nocturnal migrating birds as they strike tall, lit buildings. Not long ago, a woodcock was discovered stunned at the bottom of City Hall, and many warblers have been found dead at the foot of some of Dockland's skyscrapers each spring.

Chicago stands in the middle of a very important migratory highway, along which 5 million birds, across 250 species, fly twice a year. By 2000 Chicago's Department of the Environment estimated that tens of thousands of birds were killed from night-time lights each season. It therefore initiated the Lights Out programme, encouraging building managers to dim or turn off decorative lighting late at night and to minimise the use of interior lights during the migration season. It has subsequently won the support of the owners and managers of almost all of the major skyscrapers in Chicago.

In central London, the Illuminated River project, a large-scale art installation launched in 2016, involves lighting up bridges across the Thames. London Wildlife Trust

partnered on this project to help ensure the new illuminations are planned with the environment in mind and replace the outdated and inefficient ways the bridges were previously lit. This project also involved the first luminance studies of the Thames, to help us understand which buildings and structures are creating light pollution on the river, and how best to minimise the light spill of The Illuminated River. The project has also conducted bat and bird surveys of the riverside areas. Formerly, lighting on the bridges ran from dusk until dawn. Now all lights are switched off at 2am, and the project encourages other bridge owners to do the same to protect the darkness that is fundamental to the Thames environment.

It's not only the direct impact on wildlife but also generic light pollution that is fuelling calls for 'dark-sky places' to be created. Skyglow – the orange 'halo' over towns and roads – negates our ability to see the stars, and in many parts of London much of the stellar skyscape is obscured. Astronomers and countryside campaigners, in particular, have established the Commission for Dark Skies

(formerly the Campaign for Dark Skies) and designated a growing number of Dark-Sky Parks and Dark-Sky Reserves in Britain. While no part of London can match these, there are still significant tracts of the city where the night sky remains more ultramarine than orange, highlighting the need for their protection from development.

Within the process of development and urban design, there are positive trends that ensure light is less obtrusive, easier to control (for when it's really needed), more energy efficient and more sensitive to its impact upon bats and birds. This includes more specific control over the direction of lighting, the use of shades and the design of bulbs of specific spectral range and luminosity. These elements can be required as planning conditions to control the impact on biodiversity. Nevertheless, there are still strongly held attitudes and assumptions about lighting, especially in terms of safety, security and traffic navigation (such as, the brighter the better), that can make it difficult to balance the needs of people and wildlife in the city.

# CROSSTOWN TRAFFIC

# CROSSING THE ROAD & OTHER DIFFICULTIES

The capital is still a city of cars, although the volume of motorised traffic has been falling steadily since its peak in 1999. There are less reliable statistics about night-time road use; it seems to have risen significantly over the past 30 years, with commercial freight traffic continuing through the night (as it often used to) and starting up ever-earlier to beat the rush hour. Drivers increasingly choose to travel at off-peak times, with lifestyle factors such as leisure and flexible working also influencing this. These dampen traffic peaks but spread the 'busy-ness' of roads over a longer period of time.

Traffic levels undoubtedly have impacts on animals using roads in their nocturnal foraging. The decline of hedgehogs across London is partly attributed to traffic. Tens of thousands of hedgehogs in the country are killed by road traffic each year, and road deaths might be an important cause of their decline locally. In London, where much of the hedgehog habitat is fragmented, the cumulative impact of road deaths puts pressure on ever-smaller populations, which can become isolated and more vulnerable to local extinctions. However, the real picture is not known, and further research, which London Wildlife Trust is keen to pursue, is needed to get a better understanding of how hedgehog populations can remain viable given the increasing traffic on our roads.

Every year in March, more than 100,000 toads travel from Ham Common, Richmond-upon-Thames, to their breeding ponds on the other side of Church Road. The road is closed to drivers for three weeks to allow the toads safe passage on their 100m (109yd) journey. Volunteer 'toad-crossing' patrols are called in, armed with buckets, torches and high-visibility jackets. A volunteer gently picks a toad up by the middle and places it in the bucket, then escorts it to the other side of the road, from where it can safely make its way to the pond. The toad patrol began in 2010 and is estimated to save hundreds of toads annually.

Noise too, seems to be infiltrating the night – not only from traffic, pubs and clubs, but also from construction work, as the demands for infrastructure require 24-hour delivery programmes (with the lighting that accompanies them). In many cases the worst noise is local and temporary, and legislation is in place to limit the impact. Bechstein's bat *Myotis bechsteinii* is less likely to fly above roads than other bat species that forage in open areas, suggesting that the noise of the traffic could fragment their hunting grounds. Some birds avoid noisy areas as they cannot hear song to mark out territories or attract mates. Less clear are the cumulative effects on nocturnal wildlife – studies show that noise may alter bird breeding patterns, disturb wildlife and damage sensitive ecosystems.

# OPENING OUR EYES & EARS

It's ironic that as London has moved to become ever more busy into the night, our interest in the nocturnal wildlife we share our city with has become greater. So too, has our understanding of the impact of light and noise upon wildlife's sensitivities. In the past 30 years I've witnessed an incredible explosion of interest in bats. My first bat walk, conducted in Sydenham Hill Wood in 1991, attracted 80 people, eagerly clamouring around one primitive bat box that picked up a brief jitter of clicks that may or may not have been a pipistrelle flying above the tree canopy. It didn't matter – for most of the people joining us, it was a chance to experience the woodlands at night fully confident that they'd return home without getting lost or being attacked by a wolf. Since then, the Trust's bat walks at the Wood pick up a whole lot more bats and many more punters. Through some research conducted 20 years ago, we have established a bat roost for brown long-eared bat on the reserve, which is monitored annually.

BatFest is an annual event co-ordinated by Bat Conservation Trust and coincides with hundreds of events around the world to raise awareness of bats and their conservation needs. There's much to do still to counter bats' poor public profile (vampires and all that...). Plus there are the pressures from modern building construction squeezing out the spaces bats can use to roost – a pipistrelle needs a gap of only 8mm (just over ¼in) – and the loss of habitat on which they depend for food. This is where organisations like the London Wildlife Trust, the London Bat Group and local 'friends of parks' groups are so important in championing the needs of the city's nocturnal wildlife. In addition, there are some exciting developments in sonar and sensing technologies being developed that could help us design and manage the city for the bats into the future.

London is buzzing and will undoubtedly get busier into the night. Although we are much more aware of how this may affect our wildlife, it also faces the acute pressures of a rapidly growing city.

# Bats: it's not easy being a small bat in a big city

London is a growing city. Already home to over 9.3 million people, the capital is expanding fast. As it becomes ever more crowded, there is less and less room for wild animals and plants. While it is still a relatively green city, London's natural habitats are often small and fragmented, separated by 'barriers' of densely built-up development.

Bats, like many other species, need corridors and networks of natural habitat that allow them to move freely around an area in search of food, mates and shelter. This makes them especially vulnerable to the processes of urban densification.

Increased street lighting, depleted insect prey, high noise levels and 24-hour road traffic can also have a detrimental impact upon bats in London. However, some species do adapt to city life and they can be found in even the most built-up parts of London. A scattered network of gardens, parks, hedgerows and wilder areas provides space for commuting, foraging and sheltering bats, while areas of open water and stretches of canal provide feeding and drinking resources. London's canal network fulfils the role of a wildlife corridor, allowing bats to move deeper into the city.

Bats are widely regarded as providing a good indicator of overall landscape health and quality, being particularly sensitive to landscape change. Although bat activity is undoubtedly reduced in heavily urbanised landscapes, the presence of nine species of bat in London (out of 17 breeding species living in Britain) indicates that the city still harbours bat-friendly habitats. Daubenton's bats are particularly sensitive to higher urban densities, yet they can be seen flying in low, wide circles over waterbodies all across London. Meanwhile, pipistrelles are common in the suburbs, utilising gardens, woodland fragments and other semi-natural habitats found in outlying areas.

Gardens play an especially important role for bats in the urban landscape. They provide rich landscapes for foraging, while being ideally located to provide roosting opportunities in adjacent housing. Additionally, although lighting can be detrimental to bats, species such as noctule, Leisler's, serotine and pipistrelle have all been shown to swarm around street lighting, feasting on the insects drawn to the light.

## What do bats eat?

All British bats are nocturnal, coming out at night to feed on midges, mosquitos, flies, moths, beetles and other flying insects, which they find by using echolocation. Even the smallest of bats can eat several thousand mosquitos in a single night.

## Seeing bats for yourself

Bats can generally be seen from late March until early November in London, but this does depend on weather conditions. During the colder months, bats hibernate, slowing their heart rate right down until they are in a state of torpor. They prefer to roost in older buildings and bridges, making use of cracks, crevices and roof spaces. Modern buildings tend not to be very bat-friendly.

### BATS TO SPOT IN LONDON

*Common pipistrelle*
*Soprano pipistrelle*
*Nathusius' pipistrelle*
*Noctule*
*Leisler's*
*Serotine*
*Brown long-eared*
*Daubenton's*
*Natterer's*
*Brandt's bat and whiskered bat have also been spotted on rare occasions.*

# URBAN NATURE:
## MAKING A HOME IN THE CITY

'Only rats, pigeons and foxes' is the oft-heard layman's view on the question of London's wildlife. While these animals have marvellously adapted to the rigours of city life, for many people that is the limit of nature's inroads into the city, a perception that has only recently begun to change. London is a place largely created by and for people, and yet despite – and also because of – our endeavours, we share our city with many thousands of species of animals, plants and fungi.

So what is urban nature? In short it is the wildlife of our towns and cities, and those species that can best adapt to and flourish in the conditions found here. It is not an easy definition, as inevitably there is a spectrum of wildlife diversity that reflects the habitats and conditions found across London. In the centre it's greyer, more artificial, harsher, hotter and drier, and on the rural fringes it's greener, milder, wetter and more natural. How we manage every part of the city will influence this diversity, too.

The greatest variety of London's wildlife resides in long-standing habitats, such as old **woodlands, heaths, ponds** and **ancient meadows**, much of which survives as 'encapsulated countryside'. While these habitats are still influenced by us, they are wild places that we have never built on or changed substantially, such as **Epping Forest, Richmond Park** or **Ruislip Woods**.

Many species, however, will also be found in the countless **parks, gardens, cemeteries, canals, reservoirs, allotments** and **green spaces**, from the inner city to the outskirts. These spaces have been created, designed and managed primarily for our needs, but they also afford important places for wild animals and plants to find refuge and food and to breed.

# From here
# & everywhere

It is into such places that we have introduced hundreds of varieties of trees and plants for ornament and decoration, adding to the diversity of the city's ecology. Most of these originate from around the world, such as **rhododendron** (western China), **tree of heaven** (northeast and central China), **gum tree** (Australasia), **cedar of Lebanon** (eastern Mediterranean), **Spanish bluebell** (Spain and Portugal), **Japanese cherries** (Japan), **begonias** (Brazil) and **tulips** (Turkey), reflecting the acquisitiveness of plant collectors in the imperial adventures from the 16th century onwards.

The establishment of **botanical gardens** and **arboretums** and the subsequent democratisation of gardening from the early 20th century further led to global flora finding a home here in London. (Not all have become wild, but many have 'jumped the garden fence' to become naturalised.) The city's wildlife in the early 20th century reflected whatever had adapted to this increasingly green suburban environment.

However, a much smaller number of animals and plants could cope with the crowded, polluted conditions of the inner city, with its cramped housing, factories, railway yards, docks and wharves. The species that did were those associated with human habitats (known as synanthropic species), such as the **house mouse, black rat, brown rat, house sparrow, feral pigeon** and many **insects**. Their ability to flourish in such conditions led most of them to be considered pests and vermin. These largely unloved creatures were the urban nature of the times.

Stranger things began to occur in the mid-20th century, when London's expansion started to splutter and take a different route. The massive bomb damage from World War II was followed by the slum clearance of the 1940s and 1950s and then the creation of new towns and suburban housing estates, helping to disperse people into lower-density, greener neighbourhoods. In addition, we had started to clean our air and water, plant trees and move to a more car-based society. Industrial decline contributed to a drop in population and the creation of increasingly large expanses of wasteland and dereliction from the 1960s to the 1980s. (In 1939 London's population was 8.6 million, and in 1988 it had gone down to 6.6 million – a 25 per cent decrease in just under 50 years.)

All this created a new, post-industrial canvas for nature to exploit, often resulting in a curious mixture of wild animals and plants from Britain and the wider world. The **black redstart**, a perky central European bird, began a northern expansion in the late 19th century, and first bred in London at Wembley Park in 1926 (in one of the empty buildings from the British Empire Exhibition, which had closed in the previous year). Following the bombing of London in the 1940s, the bird had soon colonised many of the ruins, feeding on the insects attracted to the flowering weeds, such as **rosebay willowherb, mugwort** and **Canadian goldenrod**, that took root. The black redstart bred so well that it soon became known as the 'bombsite bird' (and subsequently, for similar reasons, as the 'power station bird').

## Urban wilderness

By the start of the 1980s, a lot of London was characterised by a mosaic of rough-land sites – wastes adorned with weeds, rubbish, rubble and abandoned vehicles and machinery. Much of this was around the old docklands of **Surrey Docks, the Isle of Dogs** and **Victoria Docks,** as well as abandoned railway yards, such as **Stratford, King's Cross, Willesden** and nearby **Old Oak Common, Feltham,** and **Bricklayers Arms**

**in Southwark**. These quickly became the new urban wildernesses. Many plants took to them with vigour and colour, such as **Canadian fleabane, lupin, everlasting sweet pea, mignonette, weld, wallflower, evening primrose, Italian loosestrife** and ever greater forests of **rosebay willowherb**. While some had 'leapt over the garden fence', others – through the mobility of their wind-borne seeds – could colonise such grounds with ease.

As they matured, many of the 'urban commons' matured into scrub. **Bramble** and **purple-flowered buddleia** – beloved by nectar-seeking butterflies – were among the first colonisers, liking the chemistry of mortar and concrete found on such sites. In time, many of these areas developed into woodlands of **goat willow** (pussy willow), **hawthorn, silver birch, ash, false acacia** and **sycamore**, such as those often found along railway lines. In wetter areas, dense forests of some invasive plants took root; **Himalayan balsam** ('poor man's orchid'), **Japanese knotweed** and **giant hogweed** were all originally imported for gardens but have since become problematic because they crowd out some native plants.

These rough-lands were noisy with birds, including **house sparrow, linnet, blackbird,**

**dunnock, robin** and **wren** in the lusher wildernesses, and **pied wagtail, gulls** and **crow** in the sparser derelict wastes. But their colour and buzz were provided by the insects and other invertebrates taking advantage of the nectar of the plants, the structure and refuge afforded by debris, rubble and sands, and the warmth that such grounds provide (as dark surfaces absorb the heat of the sun). Perhaps most surprising has been the importance of these urban wastelands – also known as 'brownfields' – for pollinators including a range of **bees (bumble, carder, mining, leaf-cutting), hoverflies, beetles, bugs, moths** and **butterflies**.

# Changing habitats & new arrivals

However, with the rapid growth of London since the 1990s, many of the urban wildernesses have disappeared under bricks and mortar. To counteract this, the rough, untidy character of the urban wildernesses has been replicated in 'new urban' habitats, whether as living roofs and walls on buildings or as 'pictorial meadows' in some parks. Various other strategies for urban 'greening' have also been adopted, including retrofitting filter strips (slightly sloping strips of grass) and wet or dry swales (vegetated open channels), as well as repurposing

existing green infrastructure such as verges and embankments and planting thousands of new street trees. Among the many benefits of these measures will be an improvement in London's wildlife habitats.

The city's global connections mean that London remains a key place for the arrival of many new species that have hitched lifts in cargo, in the soil on boots and tyres, or in the ballast of ships. This ecological dynamism is also affected by the climatic variations that such a huge city affords – with inner London being slightly warmer, with fewer frosts and drier summers, than the rural fringes.

What it means to be wild here will always change, but the city's urban nature is a glorious mixture of resilient natives and flexible incomers. These are the animals, plants and fungi that have been able to adapt, and they will undoubtedly continue to do so as London shifts 'from grey to green'.

# Underground mouse: burrowing deep, less sleep

The reactions of people waiting for the Tube in a London Underground station when they catch sight of some movement among the tracks are testimony of an animal's remarkable adaptability. The 'Underground mouse' is not – yet – a separate species, but it shows the extent to which nature can fill completely artificial niches.

The West European house mouse, *Mus domesticus*, is our classic synanthropic mammal – a forever busy animal that has evolved and flourished by its close association with people. Found throughout Britain, it is very common across London. It was originally from southwest Asia, but by adapting to our settlements, buildings and feeding habits, it has since spread globally and is probably the most widespread mammal around the world apart from humans.

In the past, house mice were agricultural pests. Their feeding habitats on stored grains could easily render much of the grain unusable for milling, and also contaminated other stored foods. As cities grew, house mice followed us, adapting themselves to live in plentiful family groups in the niches and crevices of our buildings, whether below

floorboards, in cellars or up in the rafters. House mice can climb, jump 60cm (2ft) and swim. There isn't anywhere far from a house mouse in London; while we have become more adept at building mouse-proof buildings, our central heating and foods will attract them. They are efficient at tunnelling, burrowing into soft earth, and by using their powerful incisors (the front chiselling teeth that define all rodents) they can chew through wood, wire and soft plastics to gain entry into places where they can nest and seek refuge.

In London they've gone one step further by occupying the warm and largely dry tunnels of the Underground. Here, where there are fewer predators but no natural light, more noise and dust, and little food, life is clearly harsher than up on the surface. Many have shorter tails, dark charcoal-grey fur (probably liberally coated in the trains' brake dust) and appear to have damaged hearing. It has been estimated that half a million Underground mice were once present throughout the tunnel network – equating to 360 mice per kilometre (580 mice per mile), although they are actually concentrated around stations and depots. However, the reduction in litter on the tracks since the early 2000s appears to have led to a drop in numbers.

'Tube mice are among the toughest of their species,' says Professor William Wisden, a neuroscientist from Imperial College London. 'They forage for food on the tracks, survive the deafening noise of the tube trains, and evade Transport for London's efforts to eradicate them.' He also suggests 24-hour tube operations will mean that the mice will 'evolve to be more stress resistant'. House mice are mainly nocturnal. Large ears and whiskers help them navigate. However, they communicate primarily by chemical means, through urine sprayed along their foraging routes; it contains proteins that help identify the gender of the originator, their health and their reproductive status. Prolific and often abundant, house mice breed around the year, but primarily over the summer months. The warmth of the Underground helps here, as well as the fact that they can breed in total darkness.

Up in the 'real world', cold weather, paucity of food and predation from rats (more so than from cats) and from some birds will result in high mortality. In addition, their country cousin the wood mouse, *Apodemus sylvaticus*, is effective in out-competing them in gardens, parks, woodland and more rural landscapes where house mice are now much less common, if not absent. However, by producing one litter (of five to eight pups) a month in good times, their populations are resilient. This evolutionary fecundity, along with their tolerance of our cities and the ability to eke out a living along the dusty, raucous tracks of the Underground, might see the emergence of a new subspecies – perhaps *Mus domestica subterraneous* – in due course.

# NOTES

## Chapter 3   BY PETER MASSINI

# CREATED SPACES

# ECOLOGY PARKS, NATURE RESERVES, CITY FARMS & COMMUNITY GARDENS

London is a created place. Ever since the Romans established the first major settlement four years after their invasion in AD43, 'Londoners' have been modifying a once wild and natural landscape to suit their own requirements. Our need for housing, transport, utilities and political and cultural institutions has supplanted nature. The built form has largely replaced natural form – a process that is, in many respects, the very essence of city-making. Nature has been deemed separate or subsidiary, conserved in set-aside places or maintaining a presence in parks and gardens created primarily for human recreation. Some species have persisted or even thrived in the ignored, unloved and unneeded parts of the city, waiting for opportunities to exploit new niches in the human-shaped landscape – opportunities that used to appear by default but more recently have done so by design.

Coinciding with the rise of environmental politics in the 1970s, and the abandonment previously industrial urban areas as the result of economic recession, many ecologists began to turn their attention towards the apparent resurgence of nature in urban environments. The gradual discovery that there were rich and ecologically significant areas of land across the city, where wildlife had retaken ground rather than remaining confined to nature reserves, made some Londoners realise that nature could be incorporated into the very fabric of the city. Harnessing the skills and experience of architects, civil engineers, landscape architects and ecologists meant that redundant spaces could be repurposed for wildlife. The created place that is London could provide new spaces for nature.

# THE FIRST
# ECO PARKS

When walking along the South Bank of the Thames between London Bridge and Tower Bridge today, it seems barely believable that this was an area of dereliction and decay in the 1970s. The glass and steel structures and limestone-led landscape of what is now More London, from where London Mayors have held sway since the opening of City Hall in 2002, were very much 'less'. With the city having barely recovered from the impact of the Blitz, the closure of London's docks in the 1960s and 1970s laid waste to the area, and the almost valueless land had been turned over to lorry parking and other temporary uses.

## William Curtis Ecological Park

Its selection as the site of London's first 'ecology park' was the result of an unlikely but happy convergence of royalty and radical thinking. The Jubilee Walkway, marking the Silver Jubilee – 25th anniversary – in 1977 of the accession of Queen Elizabeth II to the throne, was established to link the most iconic landmarks in central London. Because it had to navigate the insalubrious South Bank, something had to be done, and fast. Pioneering urban ecologists, having seen how natural processes were rapidly cloaking derelict land in a carpet of colour, convinced the powers-that-be that an ecology park would be a quick and cost-effective solution. Thus, in 1976, 900 years after William the Conqueror built his enduring fortress on the North Bank of the Thames, the William Curtis Ecological Park sprang into life as a temporary landscape on the opposite bank. It was named after the 18th century botanist who published the first comprehensive flora of London, *Flora Londinium* (1775–1796). Although this pioneering ecology park was in existence for less than ten years, it created a template that has been followed many times since, first at London Wildlife Trust's Camley Street Natural Park (see page 56) and then in those parts of London being shaped by urban regeneration.

# Eastern promise

You need to head east to discover many of London's best created places for wildlife. For generations, the flat former marshland landscapes bordering the Thames and its tributaries, such as the Lea, Beam (or Rom), Ravensbourne and Ingrebourne, downstream of Tower Bridge, were a seemingly blank and level canvas upon which successive layers of development were superimposed. Docks, factories, power stations, sewage works and scrapyards dominated parts of the riverside until economic and industrial decline resulted in the creation of wastelands and brownfields. Many of these were reclaimed by a peculiarly rich assemblage of wild and feral animals and plants.

In the late 1980s and early 1990s, these disorderly, rewilded landscapes were regarded as ripe for regeneration and redevelopment. The London Docklands Development Corporation had successfully shifted London's economic growth eastwards, and the Thames Gateway initiative aimed to consolidate that shift. New housing, transport infrastructure and logistics hubs began to transform the landscape, and slowly but surely to erase the unplanned, impulsive wildscapes regenerating behind the fenced-off, often menacing, abandoned spaces.

Though these areas, the haunts of stonechat and stonecrop, were rich in wildlife, the likelihood of retaining such apparent places of neglect amid the landscapes of renewal was a forlorn hope. It was time to apply the lessons learned at the William Curtis Ecological Park and Camley Street Natural Park, and create (or perhaps, more truthfully, shape and engineer) places for wildlife.

# Greenwich Peninsula Ecology Park

**Arriving by public transport, I emerge from the functional sterility of North Greenwich Underground station into a hardscape of glass, steel and granite.** Sometimes thronged with people bustling with excitement as they retrieve their barcodes from their mobile phones before being swallowed up by the O2 arena, this can also be a sparsely populated space. With only gulls wheeling overhead, it is animated by the brightness of the sky and the waft of the river's tidal churn – for here the Thames becomes more estuarine. A disjointed walk through expansive car parks and dizzying tower blocks, some in use and others under construction, takes you to the first created space. A carpet of grass fringed by a curtain of trees, this is a space created more for people than for wildlife. But at its southernmost reach, just beyond multicoloured blocks of apartments, I stumble onto a scene that evokes memories of childhood explorations in the secret folds of the East Sussex High Weald – I am in a wet woodland of **alder** and **willow**, through which a boardwalk leads me across a trickling, oozing woodland floor dotted yellow with **marsh-marigold**, **flag iris** and **celandine**, while **blackcaps** and **chiffchaffs** herald the arrival of spring.

This is the 'back-door' into the 2-hectare (5-acre) Greenwich Peninsula Ecology Park, on the site of an old steelworks. Created at the same time as the O2 (formerly the Millennium Dome), it is the centrepiece of the Greenwich Millennium Village, one of the first attempts at creating a more sustainable way of living in the city. Though it looks natural, the Ecology Park is actually an intricately designed and created artifice. Water levels are artificially controlled by a system of pumps and pipes and are topped up from a chalk borehole close to the park boundary. All the soils and substrates were imported or manufactured on site, allowing a mosaic of habitats including a shingle beach, reedbed and flower-rich grassland to be created alongside the wet woodland.

Returning a few weeks later, I notice from the clamour in the reedbeds and the 'kips' and 'keeyahs' overhead that the blackcaps and chiffchaffs have been joined by **reed warblers** and **common terns**. The terns had travelled further south to escape the winter winds and chill spring breezes that sweep across these former east London flatlands now becoming 'canyonised' by the tidal surge of new high-rise development.

GREENWICH MILLENNIUM
ECOLOGY PARK

It's easy to be distracted by the chatter and trill of these migratory birds, which faithfully return to this oasis despite the gradual urbanisation of the surrounding landscape. Yet it would be unforgivable to visit these east London created spaces and not pay homage to the wildlife that makes them distinctive – those opportunists, pioneers and colonists that relentlessly reclaim these spaces whenever we, by default or by design, create the conditions that allow them to thrive. These are the small or enigmatic, seldom seen things: plants like the biennial **viper's bugloss** and its attendant **mason bee** *Hoplitis adunca*. This continental species, found here in 2016, is probably dependent on the synthetic nature of the site – the unnaturally warm microclimate, the abundance of its preferred food plant and the provision of bee boxes on site which attract a wide range of mason and solitary bees. Although the viper's bugloss mason bee has not yet extended its range beyond the park, other Europeans such as **red-eyed damselfly** and **willow emerald damselfly** have used this Ecology Park and similar created places across London and the southeast as a bridgehead for more rapid colonisation of this sceptered isle.

# RIVER-HUGGING CREATED SPACES

**Emerging from the Ecology Park, I am greeted by the Thames, arguably one of the wildest and most natural parts of the capital. Even though steel piles and concrete walls constrain any landward seep of the twice-a-day tide, the grey-green North Sea ebbs and flows into the heart of the capital with untamed natural force.**

I'm heading upriver, about to soar across the Thames, to take a bird's-eye view (take your pick of peregrine, cormorant or oystercatcher who flight this stretch of the river) from the comfort of an Emirates Air Line cable car pod. But before I do, I notice a sweep of reeds softening the sea wall and lapped by ripples from the incoming tide – an unusual sight so far upriver from the reedy Kent and Essex fringes. This tide-fed rustling stand is a created space, too: an intertidal terrace carved from the former sea wall and planted with reed, sea aster and club-rush. Unlike the eco-engineered reeds of the Ecology Park, this tidal stand, known as the Estuary Edges (see page 15), backed by steel instead of willow scrub, is almost devoid of birds and other fluttering things… because it is designed for the wildlife beneath the murky waters. The closely packed stems of this Thames-side reed swamp create quiet water, a place where bass and flounder, glass eels and elvers can escape the riptides at the peak of tidal flow. The grey seal hauled out on the mudflats at the bend in the river points to the presence of its slippery prey.

It's late summer as my flight 'lands' in the Royal Docks, a large expanse of deep water that in winter might provide a refuge for diving duck if a bitter chill takes hold. But at this time of year the docks are home to thrill-seeking wakeboarders and open-water swimmers rather than great crested grebes or four-spotted chasers; for there are no edge-softening reedbeds or waterside willows here. So I head west over the Lower Lea Crossing – pedestrian- and cycle-'safe', but not pedestrian- and cycle-'friendly' – to reach the serpentine meanderings of Bow Creek, the tidal mouth of the River Lea. Here, as at Greenwich Peninsula, there is another juxtaposition of modern skyscraping London and a river-hugging created space – a metaphorical and almost literal (take a look at an aerial view) yin and yang amid the rumbling transport infrastructure of DLR viaducts and A13 river crossings.

**BOW CREEK**

# Bow Creek Ecology Park

**In the shadow of the recently developed London City Island sits Bow Creek Ecology Park, an unsung and somewhat forgotten member of the created spaces family.** A successor to the William Curtis Ecology Park and Camley Street Natural Park, but a predecessor of Greenwich Peninsula Ecology Park, it was created by the London Docklands Development Corporation in 1994. Ostensibly this was because the more intrepid ecologists exploring these parts in the late 1980s had found **hairy buttercup** *Ranunculus sardous* and other notable plants lurking amongst the flotsam and jetsam deposited by the tidal river and the ebb-and-flow of fly-tippers. In reality, Bow Creek Ecology Park was created because this narrow spit of land had no other use once it had become the platform that supports the Docklands Light Railway as it wends its way across the twisted creek from East India to Canning Town.

Irrespective of the true reasons for the establishment of this Ecology Park, it provides habitat for a different range of wildlife from the Ecological Park on the other side of the Thames. Although tightly embraced by the muddy waters of the River Lea, and without the

BOW CREEK ECOLOGY PARK

luxury of a pumped-water system like the one on the Greenwich Peninsula, it sits mostly high and dry. Consequently, the habitats are a mix of rough grassland scrub and ponds, providing home to whitethroat, linnet, grass snake and Roesel's bush-cricket. The latter, once confined to

England's south coast, has been another beneficiary of these created spaces. Aided by climate change, the usually wingless cricket has undergone a rapid expansion after gaining a foothold in frost-free urban nature parks, which provided a launch pad for the rare winged form to take flight during hot summers.

But the real surprise at Bow Creek Ecology Park is not in the park itself, but in the transition point between the created space, the engineered river wall and the natural mud and turbulence of the river. Here, especially in winter, wading birds and waterfowl such as redshank, teal and common sandpiper, more common downstream in the wilder parts of the estuary, feel secure enough to feed and roost in this hidden backwater. Kingfishers, too, can be seen, and sand martins have taken to nesting in the weep holes in the concrete retaining walls, which in turn has led to the construction of artificial sand-martin banks to encourage the establishment of more colonies of this inconspicuous cousin of the swallow and house martin. In years to come, I'll be able to follow the sand martins and kingfishers in the feeding flights upstream. Plans are in place, as part of the regeneration of this part of London, to gradually link the created spaces along the Lea, from East India Dock Basin on the edge of the Thames to the northern, wilder parts of the Queen Elizabeth Olympic Park, perhaps the best-known expression of the concept of a created space for nature.

No doubt some will see this reclaiming of land, primarily for the needs of people, as the re-taming of nature. Gone will be those abandoned landscapes where nature spontaneously returned once we had relinquished our claim. But in their place, armed with a better knowledge and understanding of how we can create spaces for nature, we can continue to connect, create and enhance urban landscapes with wilder forms of life.

# NATURE RESERVES & CITY FARMS

BY EDWIN MALINS

## Railway Fields

**Railway Fields is a Local Nature Reserve managed by The Conservation Volunteers, just off Green Lanes in Harringay, north London.** Despite the name, the dominant habitat is, in fact, secondary woodland (meaning that it has regrown naturally after being cleared in the past). The site was used as a railway goods yard until the 1960s, and it demonstrates very ably the power of nature to reclaim land as human activity ceases. Although people have become fixated on planting them, trees are capable of doing this themselves, particularly those species with wind-blown seeds such as ash, birch and sycamore.

Among the wooded areas are small meadows and a pond, which has a particularly good population of common frogs. Insects thrive in these areas that are kept open by the site's volunteers. Look out for butterflies basking in the sunlight and hoverflies holding territory in the air. Railway Fields has an unusual botanical distinction, being the only known place in the world where **Haringey knotweed** can be found, a hybrid of Russian vine and Japanese knotweed, discovered in 1987.

Railway Fields is very close to Harringay Green Lanes Overground station, while Manor House on the Piccadilly Line is also within walking distance. A visit to Railway Fields could be combined with a stroll along the Parkland Walk, which runs between nearby Finsbury Park and Alexandra Palace, or a trip to nearby Woodberry Wetlands.

# Gillespie Park

Tucked away behind Arsenal Underground station and the railway lines to the north of the Emirates Stadium is the tranquil Gillespie Park. Once railway sidings, this vital green space in the heart of an urban landscape was made possible by Islington Council and local campaigners who fought for its survival when British Rail was considering selling the land. Since the 1990s, Gillespie Park has hosted the Islington Ecology Centre, an attractive building used as a visitor and education centre focused on sustainability. This facilitates the use of the park as a resource for educating local children.

The park has a mixture of created habitat and naturally regenerated vegetation, making an interesting contrast. The meadow areas have occasional flashes of pink from grass vetchling and a **pyramidal orchid**, both unusual species of plant for Inner London. Close to a hundred species of bird have been recorded in the nature reserve, highlighting the importance of small, but ecologically rich spaces such as Gillespie Park for birds moving around the cityscape. As the area quietens down around dusk, the foxes become emboldened and can be seen strolling around the park.

A visit to Gillespie Park could either be combined with a walk to the north to Finsbury Park and the southern end of the Parkland Walk (see page 54) or by heading east to find Clissold Park or Abney Park Cemetery, both in Stoke Newington, or Woodberry Wetlands in Manor House.

# Camley Street Natural Park

Tucked away in the sliver of land between two of London's biggest railway stations – King's Cross and St Pancras – Camley Street Natural Park is both a pioneer and a stalwart of urban nature conservation. Sitting on the banks of the Regent's Canal, the site was once a coal drop, where coal would be unloaded from railway wagons onto canal barges and wagons. By the 1970s it was a derelict site and nature had taken over. Its importance and potential for wildlife in the city was recognised by campaigners, who fought for its survival against a proposal to turn it into a lorry park. In 1985 it opened as a nature reserve.

As the area of King's Cross has changed around Camley Street Natural Park over the past four decades, the nature reserve has managed to keep in touch with these changes while also being one of the only constants in the local landscape. A bridge across the canal now provides a link to the Granary Square district, and a new bespoke visitor centre in the nature reserve pays homage to the coal drops of the area's past while providing a space for learning about wildlife into the future.

On a circular walk around the nature reserve, as you go down the canal side you will pass by open meadow and pond, alive with insects in the summer. At the far end of the site, you can pause for quiet reflection on the pontoon at the water's edge. If you are lucky your reverie may be interrupted by the loud, liquid song of a Cetti's warbler hidden away in the willow. The return along the woodland part of the site gives a different feel, a soft and shady walkway through the trees. Living proof that wildlife can thrive in the heart of the city, Camley Street Natural Park offers a blueprint for similar sites that have sprung up since its inception decades ago.

# Mile End Ecology Park

Set in the wider landscape of Mile End Park, the Mile End Ecology Park is at the forefront of a new generation of urban ecology centres. At its heart is the Ecology Pavilion, which is partially buried in a grass bank and overlooks a lake complex. This earth-sheltered building with a living roof (covered with living vegetation) is one of three pavilions in Mile End Park. The design was chosen for its sustainable credentials and also as a means to add community-focused buildings to an area designated as Metropolitan Open Land. The Ecology Pavilion's glass frontage overlooks the reedbeds in the lake complex, where dragonflies and damselflies hunt among the aquatic vegetation. Waterbirds move between the lakes and the Regent's Canal, which borders Mile End Park, while garden birds dart in and out of the scrub beneath a small wind turbine.

Created alongside the canal in the wake of World War II bomb damage, Mile End Park is a linear green space that takes a landscape approach to benefit both people and wildlife. This is best exemplified by the Green Bridge that crosses the Mile End Road, which bisects the park and has grass, foliage and trees growing on it. Close to Mile End Underground station, the bridge allows pedestrians and cyclists to continue through the park at an elevated level over this busy road, but also connects the park for insects, butterflies and other wildlife which use the foliage to move from one place to another.

Mile End Park has lots of meadow areas which are good for insects, with butterflies, bees and hoverflies out visiting the flowers in the summer months. Over 400 species of beetle have been recorded in the Park, including the very rare streaked bombardier.

A visit to Mile End Ecology Park and the wider area could also encompass Tower Hamlets Cemetery Park. Designated a Local Nature Reserve, it is one of a number of old cemeteries in London that have been reclaimed by nature and now provide important wildlife habitats and green space in the city.

# Sutton Ecology Centre

Situated close to the ponds in the centre of Carshalton, south London, the Sutton Ecology Centre is a wildlife education centre with a series of habitats and demonstration gardens. Once an orchard, and then a kitchen garden for a nearby property, it opened as the Ecology Centre in 1989.

In the meadows you can hear grasshoppers in the summer months, and see butterflies on the wing feeding on the flowers. Like many such nature reserves, cuttings are composted, and the compost area provides habitat in its own right, hosting a population of slow-worm (a harmless, legless lizard).

The marsh and pond area provide habitat for aquatic insects and amphibians, and sometimes even a moorhen. These waterbirds have distinctive feathery yellow feet, and their red beaks distinguish them from their relative the coot, which has a white beak and blue-white feet.

A lavender plot is a nod to the lavender cultivation that was once common in the area. This aromatic plant is still popular with us today, but is also enjoyed by the insects that visit its flowers. Over in the woodland there is a distinctive row of Corsican pines from when the site was used as a tree nursery in the 1950s. Listen out for the trilling song of the wren, a particularly loud vocalisation for such a tiny bird. If you are lucky you may also hear the 'yaffle' of the green woodpecker, a maniacal pseudo-laughter sound, often delivered in flight.

The Sutton Ecology Centre is within walking distance of Carshalton railway station, and a visit could be combined with a trip to the peaceful nature reserve at Wilderness Island and a walk along the River Wandle as it wends its way out of Carshalton towards Morden Hall Park and Deen City Farm.

# Mudchute Park and Farm

The name Mudchute describes the process by which the nearby Millwall Dock was created in the 1860s, and silt was deposited on the land now occupied by the Park and Farm. It is in the middle of the Isle of Dogs in east London and is within walking distance of Mudchute DLR station. The Isle of Dogs has undergone significant change since the closure of London's docks between 1960 and 1980, and this open space exists thanks to the foresight of campaigners who successfully prevented the area being built on, instead creating a public park. The Mudchute Park and Farm was developed from 1977 onwards.

At 13 hectares (32 acres), Mudchute is notably large for an inner city farm, and specialises in rare breed livestock. Examples of this specialism include Dexter cattle, which is the smallest native British cattle breed, and sheep breeds such as Whitefaced Woodland and Southdown, the latter reminiscent of teddy bears. Mudchute Farm is approved by the Rare Breeds Survival Trust, an organisation that works to preserve the genetic diversity and heritage of livestock breeds across the country. Many of these breeds have fallen out of favour with contemporary commercial livestock farming and sometimes only survive in very small numbers. In recent years, sheep from Mudchute Farm have been used as a conservation tool in Green Park, as part of a trial to enhance the quality of grassland habitat there, while also providing a way for the public to connect with animals in one of central London's most high-profile parks.

There is a wide variety of habitat for wildlife across Mudchute Park. Woodlands and wetlands are intertwined with open meadows and field margins. Look out for boisterous flocks of starlings going about their daily business in typically jovial fashion. Listen carefully in case they are entertaining each other with vocal imitations of city life, such as sirens and squeaking train tracks. Flocks of goldfinches (known collectively as a 'charm') can also be seen, communicating with one another in almost electrical-sounding tweets and buzzes.

# Centre for Wildlife Gardening

Hidden away on a quiet residential street in Peckham, southeast London, the Centre for Wildlife Gardening has been providing inspiration for aspiring wildlife gardeners and schoolchildren since the late 1980s. Originally conceived as a tree nursery, the site has grown into a demonstration wildlife garden and a showcase for a variety of habitats in miniature, on a site that was once a council vehicle depot.

The entranceway is clad in hops on one side, a food plant for comma butterfly caterpillars (the adults can be seen powering their way around the site in the summer). On the other side, a toilet block cloaked in ivy provides nectar and berries late in the season and is a place to spot visiting blackcaps. A small meadow is bordered by a hedge that has been laid in a traditional style, and by an adjacent 'osier dome' which demonstrates the regenerative ability and flexibility of willows.

The largest of the site's ponds is a local hub for a large population of common toads, quite possibly one of the most significant gatherings of these fascinating amphibians in the wider area. Toads can be found in the terrestrial habitats on-site by lifting logs, or at certain times of the year out in the open hunting flying insects.

The slope below the main building is a created chalk bank, demonstrating the kind of plant communities typically found on the chalk slopes of the North Downs in Croydon and Bromley, while a nearby bed is a tribute to the oak and hornbeam woodlands of the Great North Wood that lie to the south of this wildlife garden.

East Dulwich and Peckham Rye railway stations are, respectively, five minutes' and fifteen minutes' walk away. As the garden is small, a visit could be combined with a trip to nearby Peckham Rye Park, where the River Peck briefly flows above ground, and if a longer walk is feasible, to the magnificent viewpoint over London from One Tree Hill, a woodland and Local Nature Reserve in Honor Oak.

COMMON TOAD

The large population of toads at the centre has spawned a popular event for local children known as Toad Day, to celebrate and promote understanding of these creatures.

A vision of how people and nature can exist in equilibrium right in the middle of our capital city.

# Phoenix Garden

**The Phoenix Garden has been a part of the fabric of Covent Garden since the 1980s. It is located behind the Phoenix Theatre in Stacey Street, where it occupies a former World War II bomb site that had subsequently been used as a car park.** As a result, the garden's underlying soil is very thin and mostly composed of rubble. This makes it quite a dry environment, which when combined with the warmer ambient temperature of the city centre enables an interesting range of plants to thrive. Perhaps one of the most notable examples is the giant viper's bugloss, a plant endemic to La Palma, one of the Canary Islands, but providing the nectaring insects of Phoenix Garden with a colossal vertical buffet.

The garden has the West End's only population of **common frog**, as well as a suite of garden birds. The success of this small site in attracting wildlife is the direct result of its management ethos of minimal intervention. A visit to Phoenix Garden challenges our perceptions and categorisations of the natural world. What is a weed? What is a pest? Do we need to water everything, or can we allow the climate and soil to dictate the range of plants that grow?

Phoenix Garden provides an interesting and important contrast with some of the more manicured parks and gardens within its West End orbit, and perhaps a vision of how people and nature can exist in equilibrium right in the middle of our capital city.

# South London Botanical Institute garden

**Based in a large but unassuming Victorian house in Tulse Hill, the South London Botanical Institute is a fascinating place to visit for those of all ages and backgrounds with an interest in plants.** Founded in 1910, the Institute welcomes people of all levels of skill and knowledge to learn about botany and the wider natural environment, through its school visits, talks, workshops, group tours, library, herbarium and garden.

The Institute's garden is both meticulously organised and packed out, with over 500 labelled species. It can be visited whenever the building is open or for special garden open days and evenings. Particular attention is paid to plants that are less often celebrated, an example of which is a dedicated Weed Bank. Themed beds feature drought-tolerant, scented, medicinal dye and other plants and there are small collections of ferns, mosses, carnivorous and poisonous plants. Given that much of the work of the Institute involves teaching people to recognise the plants all around them, those native to the British Isles are given equal billing with exotica from around the world.

Another interesting area is Gerard's Border, a bed dedicated to the plants recommended by John Gerard of Holborn in his seminal 1597 book *Herball*. The work detailed herbal remedies for common illnesses of Tudor times, and this border features a number of these plants, many of which remain common across London and the wider countryside to this day.

The pond in the centre of the garden is a showcase for British wetland plants such as bogbean, brooklime and marsh-marigold. It has a particularly vivacious population of common frogs and smooth newts who delight visiting groups of schoolchildren as well as adults seeking peace and tranquillity in beautiful, botanical surroundings.

THE GARDEN GREENHOUSE

COMMON FROGS

DEADLY NIGHTSHADE, *ATROPA BELLADONNA*

**Themed beds feature small collections of ferns, mosses, carnivorous and poisonous plants.**

The farm has a range of animals from rabbits to donkeys, with the sheep and goats particularly visible to passers-by in the park.

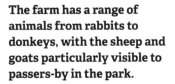

# Hackney City Farm

**Hackney City Farm is on Goldsmiths Row, in the southeast corner of Haggerston Park near Hoxton, east London.** Inspired by the success of the Kentish Town City Farm, Hackney City Farm was set up in 1984 to give an opportunity for the local community to experience farming. The farm has a range of animals from rabbits to donkeys, with the sheep and goats particularly visible to passers-by in the park.

The farm has Tamworth pigs, an old English breed descended from the wild boar that would have roamed the European wilderness (most modern pig breeds have some east Asian ancestry). It is this link to wild boar that has resulted in Tamworths being used at the Knepp Wildland rewilding project in West Sussex, and the two Tamworths at Hackney City Farm are among the star attractions.

The farm also has a garden which features herb beds, a bog garden for wetland plants and an orchard. Although primarily established in urban areas as part of food growing projects such as this, community orchards will, over time, become fantastic resources for wildlife. Fruit trees reach veteran status much faster than longer-lived tree species, supporting a wide array of insect life in their cavities, rot holes and sap runs.

A trip to Hackney City Farm might also encompass a visit to the famous Columbia Road Flower Market nearby (only operating on Sundays), as well as a stroll along the Regent's Canal to the east towards Victoria Park. Spitalfields City Farm is also fairly close by to the south.

# Vauxhall City Farm

**London's most central city farm was founded in the 1970s as part of wider protests by the North Lambeth Neighbourhood Council against the demolition of local buildings. The farm sprung up on vacant land as a community project.**

As with many city farms, the animals may appear to be the principal focus but they are, of course, a vehicle for community and educational projects. Some of the animals that immediately catch the eye of passers-by are the goats, pigs and sheep. The farm also has three alpacas, called Tom, Ben and Jerry. The farm also engages in promoting local wildlife and plant life by creating programmes aimed at connecting their community with the environment around them.

Vauxhall City Farm overlooks the adjacent Vauxhall Gardens, a public park that was the site of the famous pleasure gardens of the mid-17th to mid-19th centuries, and some of the farm's paddocks are effectively in the park. If you head past the pond and the avenue of cherry trees towards the sports courts, there are a number of elm trees. Although mature English elms are a thing of the past in London as a result of Dutch elm disease, these resistant cultivars are thriving. In their canopy lives the elusive **white letter hairstreak** butterfly, possibly the most central population of this species in London. Its caterpillars feed on the flowers, seeds and leaves of the elms, and the adults feed on honeydew, a sugary substance produced by aphids. The adults fly in July and are difficult to spot but can be seen flitting in and out of the canopy on warm evenings.

A visit to Vauxhall could also include a walk around nearby Bonnington Square, where there is a heady mix of tropical planting on the streets. The community garden is a legacy of squatters in the 1980s seeking to save the buildings from demolition and foster a community spirit, much like Vauxhall City Farm's founding ethos.

The farm engages in promoting wildlife and plant life by creating programmes aimed at connecting their community with the environment around them.

# COMMUNITY GARDENS

BY SOURABH PADKE

As a newcomer to London, I was reassured by the gardens and parks that are sprinkled across the urban fabric. The space to breathe, to consider, to ponder and to be is always welcome (as is the knowledge that I'm never too far from a benevolent tree). As a schoolteacher back in India, gardens presented themselves as the ideal bridge to span the polarities of the abstract and personal experience. We are able to draw from an inheritance and to pass on that which we consider to be of value. It brings us together for collective experience and nudges us towards considered action. It is this garden of ideas that I intend to peruse through.

OSBORNE CLOSE, HERNE HILL

The word 'garden' can evoke an array of visions in our minds. It could be a serene sanctum sanctorum, a blaze of flowers, a hive of hyperactive bees, a fragrant corner to relax in the company of a good book (or a close friend), a vibrant source of fresh food or even a place to break a sweat in productive labour. It is safe to say that the garden is a space for the senses and one that is meant to offer experiences and evoke memories.

# COLLABORATION WITH
# THE PAST & THE FUTURE

As an act, gardening is embedded in our humanity. It is a perennial ritual that has been passed down through millennia and scores of generations. A practice that unites humans across cultures and yet, for all its global presence, is an acutely contextual and local dialogue that stays true in every moment. It is the perpetuation of a virtuous cycle of care and exchange. You care for the garden, the garden cares for you.

In a sense, the term 'community gardening' could be considered a tautology. Every act of gardening simply cannot be done without a community. Gardening is a collaboration across time, space and life. It has taken millennia for the mighty elements to grind the mountains down to dust. Lives beyond number had to live and die to mingle with this mountain dust. What we today call soil is one of the longest community projects of which we, too, are a part. Our ancestors took time to befriend plants that were carefully chosen and encouraged to produce particular results. The seeds we plant today are our collective inheritance, and our actions are the ways in which we choose to collaborate with future generations. Fellow creatures, ranging from bacteria and fungi to earthworms and snails, and to the birds and the bees, are all our teammates working on this magnificent collective effort. Even today, not a single garden could exist for long if this fellowship drifted apart. To garden is to participate in this venture with an awareness of the limited stake and control we have in the process. It is trust, gratitude and surrender that help us become equal participants in the process.

A project so inherently collective is also the perfect habitat for people to come together in solidarity. Community gardens have something to offer everyone. We know how to garden together even if we haven't done it yet. People of all ages and abilities can engage meaningfully with and within gardens. There's always somebody else who resembles us, making the process feel even more familiar. Be it the baby seedlings and saplings that need gentle care, or the withering leaves that depart from the tree and are gathered together; the tendrils that reach out into the unknown in search of support, or the fibrous roots mirroring the same in an attempt to stay grounded. There's birth and death, growth and decay, ambition and helplessness, prickly thorns and velvety leaves – all in one place, just like within ourselves.

The nature of the task at hand encourages us to forge friendships and to move together with a sense of purpose. In that sense, community gardening is very much like any other team sport. The rules of the game here are literally the laws of nature, and the repercussions of gardening can be felt at three progressive, overlapping levels: interpersonal, intrapersonal and impersonal.

# INTERPERSONAL: COMMON GROUND

# INTRAPERSONAL: LOOKING WITHIN

A garden tends towards the collective. It both asks for and gives back in a manner that defeats any notions of individuality and ownership. The process covers the full gamut of cooperation, from the conscious care and effort needed for digging, sowing, cutting, transporting, storing and cleaning (all of which benefit from many hands) to the copious bounties of food, fodder, fuel and friendship (which are meant to be shared). The same garden can be an overwhelming chore for one but a joyous ritual for many.

Gardens teach us to ask for help, to reach out. They provide a space where a variety of people, with a range of interests, can work differently and yet as a part of the same collective. Everyone can find their own way of doing the same thing, which paves the way for understanding, sharing, solidarity and relationships. It's the ideal glue to hold a community together! Since the nature of the collaboration is non-competitive, cooperative, egalitarian and productive, a community garden is a welcoming space for everyone to join in and to participate.

A garden moves at its own pace. The natural rhythm resonates with corresponding cycles of the sun, moon and earth. This real-time motion is an opportunity for us to align our own rhythm with it. To slow down. It is only when water stops flowing that it can soak into the earth beneath. Similarly, when we slow ourselves down to nature's pace, we can allow life to seep into ourselves. It becomes easier to hear our own thoughts and feelings when they don't have to shout over each other for an audience.

Being in this natural space and time creates patterns that mirror each other naturally. As we water the plants, we pause to water those parts of ourselves that need attention. In the same way as we gather and compost leaf litter, we collect and process our memories. When we plant a seed in the ground, we plant our aspirations for the future. We tend, we maintain and we replenish. We cultivate the garden and the self, together.

# IMPERSONAL: WHAT'S WITHIN IS WITHOUT

# A DIALOGUE BETWEEN NATURE & CULTURE

Much of modern life seems to affirm the unquestioned importance of the self. We are progressively weaned off our communal selves towards an ideal that's isolationist and lonely. Every act of ours seems to tangle us up in this web further and tighter, until we can only identify within ourselves. Me.

But a garden allows me to see how everything in nature behaves like me, giving rise to the possibility of seeing the corollary: I behave like everything else in nature. I am natural. I am nature! What I believed to be my unique actions, feelings, aspirations and tendencies seem to be shared by everything and everybody else in nature.

This realisation allows us, for a moment, to step out of our shoes and to walk lightly and truly. It is a small yet significant step in a spiritual journey that is free of any baggage and leads us towards our true collective nature.

Community gardens thus occupy the space between what we perceive as 'human culture' and the corresponding 'other' which we refer to as 'nature'. This in-between space is critical, for it serves as a way of bridging the two – to invite nature for a dialogue with culture. It is this dialogue that manifests itself as gardens, affecting both sides immensely, just as we have already witnessed the ripples caused on the human side of things.

In ecocentric terms, gardens are especially critical in urban agglomerations, to provide habitats, corridors, nesting niches, pollination pods, organic matter, groundwater replenishment and space for all the stakeholders in the landscape.

It is only when culture accommodates nature that we can attain a balanced existence. It affords us the space to consider and re-evaluate aspects of our society that we take for granted. It could be our unbridled hunger for resources, our over-reliance on industrial, post-industrial and virtual forms of personal fulfilment, our increasing identification as consumers instead of producers, our emphasis on impersonal or analytical thinking which may deprive us of a wholehearted engagement, or the fractured nature of society.

# LONDON'S BIGGEST ASSET

Of course, a garden isn't a magic pill for treating these societal ailments, but they could simply be an indicator of our collective commitment to building a more compassionate culture – one where we make time and space for ourselves and each other in order to engage with what we value. So a community garden isn't a space or a project so much as a declaration of intent. It is a signal that we are affirming our will to come together and work towards creating something that transcends us all. We slowly evolve from being just city dwellers to becoming citizens. Far from being bubbles we live in, separate from the outside world, gardens provide opportunities for engagement, discussion, decision-making, deliberation and negotiation. All of these aspects of communication are critical if we are to turn what could be likened to a bunch of tangled threads into a woven fabric in which the strands interact and strengthen each other.

Which brings us to London. This city is an incredibly complex and rich ecosystem. Its location along the Thames and its sheer size, incorporating a variety of habitats, create a strong basis for such a transformation. Today London is a critical node in the network of resources, be they of matter, energy or people. This affords London (and Londoners) exposure and access to a multitude of materials, technologies, products, services and cultures. In turn, the cultures explode into a kaleidoscope of languages, clothes, foods, stories, arts, paradigms, approaches, morals and potentially gardens.

The key advantage here is diversity, crucial for the health of any ecosystem. It is diversity that offers a system or a culture a variety of opinions to consider and use to forge ahead. Any ecosystem – including human society – that tends towards a monoculture moves along a downward spiral towards collapse. A diverse ecosystem, on the other hand, is robust and resilient in the face of inevitable change. London's diversity is its biggest asset, albeit one that could be realised further. A random collection of musicians doesn't ensure an instant symphony. Dialogue, an exchange, solidarity and the cultivation of a shared intent of harmony are necessary preludes to any such occurrence. There needs to be a collective and intentional act of care. In other words, gardening needs to take place.

So how do we garden London is a question that needs to be answered at multiple levels and collectively. How do we navigate this incredible sea of people and harness its vibrant energy, how do we turn numbers of humans into a network of communities? How could we imagine this singular organism? One definite path is via community gardens. As the name suggests, there's two simultaneous processes taking place. A community partakes in the process of gardening and in the same breath a community is being gardened. Just like an 'Apple farm' grows apples, a 'Community Garden' cultivates community.

What we need is a citywide movement that harnesses open spaces as conscious opportunities to bring people together for a cause that touches each and every one of us

at a gut level, quite literally. This could be a way of engaging people with the land they stand on, to have a full bodied say in their lives and to feel grounded. Open spaces can be watered with our attention to create a bloom of beauty, ownership and sheer joy of sharing a common legacy. Legacy is a heavy word. It reaches out into the unknown future fearlessly, knowing that what is being done now will add value to the lives of those who come after us. Community Gardens will create flowers, food and friendship for now, but more importantly they will cultivate a compassionate culture that we can sow collectively so that our future can reap its benefits.

# Hedgehogs: how to help them in your garden

**Ensuring that a city has healthy, connected wildlife habitats is the essential first step in helping a local hedgehog population recover. But we can't do it alone – everyone who lives in London has a part to play. To save the hedgehog, we need people to work together with their neighbours on small changes that will make a big difference. This is crucial because no garden or green space can help hedgehogs in isolation, but when they are linked together hedgehogs can thrive in any location.**

Hedgehogs need to be able to roam far and wide in search of food, mates and nesting sites. Get together with your neighbours to cut 13cm (5in) holes at the bottom of your fences, or dig channels beneath your garden boundaries to connect the gardens. You can then add your hedgehog hole to our national network (see References & resources, page 190).

Ditch the slug pellets and avoid the use of pesticides. Hedgehogs are natural pest controllers and need a plentiful and varied supply of invertebrate prey to stay healthy. Although hedgehogs are great swimmers, they can sometimes struggle to climb out of steep-sided ponds, and many will drown. Either provide a ramp for them, made from a plank wrapped in chicken wire, or create shallow areas at the edge of the pond so they can scramble out.

Check for hidden hedgehogs before lighting bonfires, strimming or mowing the lawn. Keep plant netting, tennis nets and household rubbish above ground level to prevent hedgehogs from getting caught in them.

Log and leaf piles, wilderness areas and purpose-built hedgehog homes make great places for hedgehogs to nest and hibernate. Fallen leaves are the perfect nesting material, so make sure you don't clear all of these away.

Attract plenty of natural hedgehog food by keeping your garden diverse, with a variety of habitats such as ponds, log piles, hedges and a wide range of plant types. Don't be afraid to let your grass grow a little wild and leave some leaf litter, as both are important homes for the hedgehog's prey. Living in an urban area needn't mean that you can't help the hedgehog.

## WHAT HAS CAUSED HEDGEHOGS TO DECLINE IN THE CAPITAL?

◆ *Lifeless gardens: Increased paving, decking, artificial lawns and tidier, less natural gardens all contribute to the loss of London's hedgehog habitat.*

◆ *Barriers to movement: More fences and busier roads make it harder for hedgehogs to hunt for food – and find a mate – while also making movement more dangerous.*

◆ *Decline in prey: With falls in the numbers of many of the small animals that hedgehogs eat, such as beetles and other insects (caused in large part by the use of pesticides), there is an inevitable knock-on effect.*

## WHAT DO I DO IF I FIND A SICK OR INJURED HEDGEHOG?

If you're concerned about hedgehogs that are underweight or are active in winter, provide tinned cat or dog food and fresh water. The British Hedgehog Preservation Society can offer advice and help you find a rescue centre near you (see References & resources, page 190).

# NOTES

## Chapter 4    BY TIM WEBB

# THE GLORY
# OF PARKS

# WHERE NATURE RULES

'Parks are the lungs of London' is a statement you
will often hear. To me, parks are the unwritten history
and culture of the people who have lived, worked and
relaxed in them and the societies behind their creation.
Parks are where nature rules and where I can forage
for berries, herbs or mushrooms. They are the spaces
where we play and meet, often lounging on the grass
on a summer's evening with good food, a nice drink and
the gentle buzz of conversation while the underlying
laughter of children spills over from the playground.

# WHAT DO WE
# MEAN BY PARKS?

**AN ATMOSPHERIC**
**AUTUMN MORNING**
**IN HACKNEY DOWNS PARK**
If I were a fox, parks would
be my larder, my school and
my home once the noise,
bustle and most of the light
had gone. A place to dig holes,
frolic with siblings, find
a mate, raise a cub or two
or bark and scream at the
moon. Any pools or fountains
would provide water. The
hedges, trees and other plants
harbour food, but so, too, do
the bins or the rubbish left by
two-legged visitors. Daytime
is set aside for resting.

As a rook or a carrion crow,
I'd be perched high up in a
mature tree in my stick-built
nest, safely surveying the
scene. Occasionally there
would be a jay, a magpie or,
more likely these days, a
ring-necked parakeet to chase
away. Food would come in the
shape of eggs of other birds,
insects or worms in the grassy
playing fields or meadows,
and any scrub would provide
berries or seeds. Then there's
food left by people, too.

Parks belong not just to us all, but also to the plants, bugs, birds and other creatures that live there. Before we get too embroiled by the wildlife, let's first consider what we mean when talking about parks. They largely consist of the more formalised and designed green spaces of the city, such as playing fields, squares, commons, playgrounds, some cemeteries, as well as the more 'typical' parks, from those of Victorian origin to those created in the past 50 years. Many have wild corners; some are much more naturalised than others. There are complex designations important to greenspace managers and planners, such as Historic Parks & Gardens, Metropolitan Open Land, District Parks, and Local Green Space.

Sometimes a park is a remnant of an ancient estate, forest or royal hunting ground. Some are built on plague pits. Charterhouse Square was London's biggest plague pit, with some 50,000 bodies buried there in the 17th century. Today it is a 2-hectare (5-acre) pentagonal garden square at the boundary of Islington and the City of London. Other parks are part of chalk downland, World War II bomb sites or abandoned warehouses, factories, orchards, reservoirs or rail infrastructure. Parks are open public spaces, free for anyone to enjoy, and there are more than seven thousand of them within the M25 London Orbital Motorway. Every single one is unique.

Victoria Park is often cited as the capital's first official park. It was created in Hackney in 1842, and similar designs followed in Battersea, Finsbury and Southwark. The 2.2-hectare (5½-acre) Finsbury Circus Gardens in the City of London dates back to 1607, when it was called Moor Fields, and claims to be London's first public park. The present garden was originally laid out in 1815.

# A MULTITUDE OF USES

Victoria Park and its cousins were created for the working classes as spaces where they could relax and exercise. This theme now seems remarkably familiar to us since Covid-19 humbled the world and forced us to retreat into our homes. Parks became the only social place outside of our homes where we could all visit regularly, for relaxation and exercise. But the pandemic revealed a societal imbalance. It brought into stark focus the shameful overlap between areas of low income and high Covid death tolls, with areas where there were few green spaces. This evidence should lay to rest once and for all any doubts of the importance of access to parks for public health.

Parks are places for innovation, too. In the 19th century, London's pleasure gardens were famous worldwide. They served as art galleries, fashion shows and engineering marvels, and led to the first development of mass catering, outdoor lighting, public balloon flights, orchestrated firework displays and much, much more. These were outdoor spaces made for mass entertainment, where people from all classes mixed for fun and quite a lot of debauchery. Pleasure gardens were very much spaces for people, but strange, exotic plants and animals were welcome in the pastoral setting of orchards, green meadows and risqué hedged gardens for secret assignations!

Today's parks are no less innovative. Some are being developed as power stations, others as climate-control machines or multi-use spaces for outdoor working. This needs some explaining.

The power stations are not giant, smoke-belching buildings sprouting chimneys and shiny tubes. These are ground-source heat pumps with underground pipes capturing a degree or two difference in temperature to heat nearby homes or generate electricity. The pipes are laid without excavating the surface, so on the ground the park is unchanged and tree roots are avoided.

Parks are effectively natural climate-control machines. The trees and other plants produce oxygen, absorb pollution and modulate climate and humidity. In summer, the tree canopies provide shade to keep us cool and act as windbreaks in stormy weather. During rainy seasons, they capture rainwater and reduce the run-off that would otherwise cause localised flooding.

With more people willing and able to work from home, the way we live is changing. Some new developments are predicated on the belief that first-time buyers will want to eat out, play out and work out. As a result, homes are smaller and facilities like restaurants, outdoor gyms and smart parks (with wi-fi, charging points and plenty of meeting areas) are a must.

**HYDE PARK**

# DOES NATURE SHAPE OUR PARK LANDSCAPES OR DO PEOPLE?

The flavour of a park is shaped by the events and actions local communities pursue, and every park is unique in what it gives to its local community by way of the nature it supports. There are lots of other factors, too, such as the quality and type of soil and underlying substrates (plenty of London clay but also sand and chalk, depending on where you are in London); the location of ponds, streams and trees; and the park's elevation and whether it gets morning, evening or all-day sunshine.

Having said all that, London's newest, biggest park, the **Queen Elizabeth Olympic Park in Stratford**, was carved into the landscape that was previously taken up by light industry, manufacturing and warehouses built for jobs long faded from memory, like making matches or bars of carbolic soap. Quite a bit of the soil was toxic and

**QUEEN ELIZABETH OLYMPIC PARK**

covered by concrete, and the area was carved up by major roads, canals and rail lines. Now it has woodlands, reedbeds that are part of a sustainable drainage system linked to the adjoining housing, wildflower meadows and tiered gardens with playgrounds, climbing walls, unrivalled sporting facilities and barbecue areas.

Parks are urban creations and so are shaped by people. But the best parks are shaped by people informed by nature, for people who enjoy being outdoors surrounded by natural beauty. Is a park with no flowers really a park? **Green Park**, adjoining **St James's Park**, was flower-free for some time, with closely cropped grass and well-pruned trees and hedges. But even here there are now flowers. We have come to realise the power and value of letting nature into our lives.

NORTHALA FIELDS SITS ALONGSIDE THE BUSY A40 AT NORTHOLT AND CONSISTS OF THREE CONICAL MOUNDS BUILT FROM CLEAN CONSTRUCTION WASTE FROM THE OLD WEMBLEY STADIUM AND NEARBY WESTFIELD SHOPPING CENTRE.

# PUSHING THE BOUNDARIES

Long before Kew Gardens built its iconic giant heated glasshouse in west London, other large glasshouses existed in east London. Joachim Conrad Loddiges was the son of a German gardener working for a nobleman near Hanover. Conrad came to England in the mid-18th century and bought a small nursery near the Hackney Empire Theatre on Mare Street. He became a world-leading importer, discoverer and recorder of plants. His heated glasshouses recreated some of the steamy habitats his imported plants needed to grow. Today, there is no trace of Loddiges's amazing nursery, but specimens from Hackney helped establish Kew Gardens. Loddiges and Sons provided trees and plants for parks and garden squares across London and the whole country.

Conrad's son, George, supplied trees for Abney Park Cemetery in Stoke Newington, which was Europe's largest arboretum at the time, with 2,500 specimens. You can still explore the surviving trees and shrubs of this amazing landscape project by visiting the cemetery, one of London's 'magnificent seven' Victorian cemeteries. It's alive with history and wildlife including foxes, small mammals, owls, those ever-present ring-necked parakeets and a wealth of birds amid the bramble, ivy, fungi, mosses, flowers, monuments and memorials.

SOCIAL DISTANCING REMINDER SPRAY-PAINTED ON A PARK PATH. ONE DAY PEOPLE WILL SEE THE INDISTINCT TRACE OF THIS AND WONDER WHAT IT MEANT.

When you scratch the surface of modern global issues like pandemics and climate change, you will find common ground. Key aspects can be addressed by adopting nature-based solutions – approaching the challenges from the perspective of the natural world. New policies and legal, scientific and behavioural changes are obviously needed, too, but working with nature is crucial. More and more people live in cities where we rely on parks and privately owned gardens for nature. These spaces will provide the foundations of a better, more resilient London where life is greener, healthier and wilder.

It is a sad fact that there is not enough public green space in London, and that much of what there is could be far better in terms of biodiversity. Why corporations and financiers, especially risk-management experts from the insurance world, are not falling over themselves to invest in this sector is a mystery.

Conversations I have had with leading assessors and city analysts quickly find common ground on how investment in quality green space can reduce payouts from insurers for health and property claims, while also creating new jobs and better living standards. Who is not mystified when considering the low bank balances of the charities and organisations struggling to deliver the very goals that investors want to see? With just modest investments they deliver remarkable results yet struggle to raise funding for core costs. Economists recognise that a diversified portfolio of investments is more resilient to sudden economic shock, and the same is true of diverse nature. The richer it is, the faster it bounces back from catastrophe. I am sure there is an analogy here involving eggs and baskets. Feel free to make up your own and jot it in the margin.

There has been much talk of rewilding habitats. This is where typical land management of an area is suspended and nature is given a freer hand to evolve, often with the reintroduction of lost species such as otters or wild boar in Britain, wolves and bears in other parts of the world. It's not really feasible to rewild London in the same way, but we can rewild our approach to nature. Let's not forget, a human being is just another animal. What if we all started growing plants on our windowsills, balconies and roofs, or adopting tracts of land to plant fruit or vegetables. Some other cities have started licensing systems for citizens keen to green their neighbourhoods. It's a rewilding of people's minds and thought processes, reconnecting them with the nature in our parks.

What if our office blocks had cloaks of trees, shrubs and hanging plants, and our streets were transformed from grey tarmac to grass and wildflower meadows? Barcelona in Spain is trying this sort of approach. It's built on a grid system so its easier to identify areas where this can happen while allowing clear routes for utility, emergency, delivery and domestic vehicles. These green grids could easily link to parks via green walkways and bridges so that people and wildlife could move without barriers such as busy roads.

The UK Government is coming under pressure to adopt a better measure of success

## AN EVER-CHANGING CAST OF CHARACTERS

than Gross Domestic Product (GDP). A 2021 independent review, *The Economics of Biodiversity: The Dasgupta Review*, argues that nature is an asset, like roads, health, knowledge, income and profit. A measurement of 'natural capital' based on indicators like land quality, species abundance and green space alongside GDP is the solution being proposed. There is a debate about putting a cash value on nature, but when you consider that global capital per person increased by 13 per cent between 1992 and 2014, while natural capital declined by 40 per cent per person in the same period, anyone can understand that our existing systems do not balance.

Transformational change is required on a global level. Protecting our oceans, tropical rainforests and marshlands is where governments come in. On a local level, that change will come through our behaviour and our parks and gardens. I believe I am of the first generation where my daughters will inherit a world poorer in wildlife, plants and habitats than the world I inherited from my parents. This change has been long and slow in coming and will now take a long time to slow down. Nevertheless, as an optimist, I remain positive that the decline can be reversed.

**So back to parks and how awesome they are. A good park can boost the physical and mental health of visitors. It can lift spirits and reduce anxiety. For every £1 invested in parks, society is estimated to get a £27 return. Changing daily through the seasons, a park can go from a winter wonderland to a warm, lazy summer garden. It features an ever-changing cast of characters (people and wildlife) and a backdrop you couldn't recreate on a stage, from the snowdrops of late winter and the daffodils of spring, through the wildflowers of summer and the fiery-coloured leaves of autumn.**

The top three most commonly seen creatures in our parks these days are **grey squirrel**, **pigeon** and **ring-necked parakeet**. In the mid-1970s, house sparrows were the most common urban species, with a count in Kensington Gardens recording 2,500 house sparrows. When the same survey was conducted again in the year 2000, not a single **house sparrow** could be found. In the 1980s, pigeons became the bird that people would interact with instead of the sparrow. In the 1990s, visitors to St James's Park posed for photos as they held out nuts or bread for grey squirrels (the sparrows having long gone). These days, the creature most likely to interact with people in those same central London parks is the ring-necked parakeet.

While noisy, bright green parakeets are easy to spot, smaller birds like **wren, house sparrow, tits** and even **thrushes** are less obvious. These other species are also less likely to interact with people in the same way as a pigeon or squirrel. **Ducks, moorhens** and **coots** will come towards you for bread but won't perch on your arm like sparrows used to.

The biggest creatures in our parks are **deer, donkeys** and **goats** in enclosures. But there is far more life present than you are likely to see on a casual stroll. Invertebrates make up 97 per cent of all life on earth and have been around for some 480 million years. We humans only turned up about three million years ago. I quizzed the Earthworm Society a couple of years ago on how many **earthworms** live in London. They estimated that soil of average quality, typical of our

TOP ROW: PARAKEET; RED DEER; MEADOW CORAL BOTTOM ROW: KESTREL; SMALL TORTOISESHELL BUTTERFLY; HONEYBEE

parks, could support as many as eight million worms in a hectare (which is over three million in an acre). At the time, that was about the same as the entire human population of the capital.

There are much smaller things in our parks and green spaces, including all manner of **fungi** and **mosses**, but also bacteria and microorganisms. There's a whole army of detritivores (creatures that consume detritus such as decomposing animals and plants), like **woodlice** and **earwigs**, turning fallen leaves and other decaying matter into healthy soil. However, because the Covid-19 lockdowns led to a large increase in park visitors, using paths that were often too narrow to accommodate the volume of people present, the grassy areas either side of the paths became muddy borders of compacted soil in which there was little life. Restoring these areas takes time, effort and some respite from being walked on.

Large, informal parks like Hampstead Heath, with its meadows, ponds, woodland, scrub, shrubs and gardens, are home to a great variety of wildlife, including **grass snake, signal crayfish, kingfisher, kestrel** and **owls**. Hampstead Heath has London's largest population of **hedgehogs**, and they are also found in other parkland including Regent's Park, Barnes Common and Putney Common. But whereas London had an estimated 30 million hedgehogs in the 1950s, today that figure is believed to have shrunk to under a million.

London's parks also attract large numbers of migrant species, from **painted lady butterfly** and **robin to ladybirds, swift, redwing and swallow**. With our changing climate, we will no doubt get to see the punky-looking **hoopoe** vying for position with green woodpeckers on park meadows or playing fields, using their pointy beaks to wheedle out ants from the grass.

TOP ROW: MULBERRY TREE, FORTY HALL; WATER VOLE; JACKDAW
BOTTOM ROW: SIGNAL CRAYFISH; GREY SQUIRREL; GRASS SNAKE

There are dozens of pollinators, too, including vast numbers of domesticated **honeybees** from hives on rooftops, walls or back gardens. Beekeeping has become big business in the capital. Wild bees have to compete with these farmed cousins, so any new sources of nectar are most welcome. **Wasps** are as important as bees for pollinating many of our plants and fruit trees.

**Mulberry trees** are dotted all around London's parks, and their history tells a tale dating back to their introduction into Britain by the Romans. Apart from their fruit, mulberries were treasured for their role in the silk industry. In the early 17th century, King James I of England was so taken with the idea of having English silk that he asked the nobility to plant ten thousand mulberry trees. Sadly, he got the species wrong as it is the leaves of the white mulberry that the larvae of *Bombyx mori*, the silk moth, devour. Most of London's mulberries are black.

**Water voles** used to be relatively common in parks and along London's waterways. Most were lost to predation or pollution in the 1990s, but some remain, especially in protected areas like Walthamstow Marshes, Rainham Marshes, Osterley Park and Crane Park, and a reintroduction programme is underway to bring them back to the Hogsmill River in Kingston upon Thames.

Our parks and green spaces are also home to 'Marmite species' – creatures you either love or hate. Sadly, water voles can look a little like rats, which puts a lot of people off. Rats aren't alone in being perceived as antisocial neighbours. They are joined by **foxes, grey squirrels, magpies, crows, those noisy ring-necked parakeets, snakes, spiders** and **mosquitoes**. Ongoing monitoring of mosquitoes in our parks has found that most of the UK's 30 different species are present in the capital and do not cause major harm here. The monitoring would pick up on any carrying harmful disease or viruses.

Getting close and truly discovering what is in your park takes time and patience. The Friends of Warwick Gardens describe the park they care for as Peckham's premier 24-hour municipal open space. Sound enticing? Penny Metal is a graphic designer who went on a mission with her camera and over the course of six years recorded 555 different species in Warwick Gardens' 1.52-hectare (3¾-acre) space. And that's just the insects. Her book is astonishing and hilarious, as is the online version (see references & resources, page 190). Check out the image of the **figwort weevil** that Penny named Jeremy. It's a magnificent shot and you can almost hear a mumbled grumble as you look at this tiny creature, bent over on its haunches while perched on a leaf.

# LOOKING AFTER OUR PARKS

# THE FUTURE OF LONDON'S PARKS

The management and care of parks and gardens is a complex mass of relationships and interconnected organisations involving a small number of paid – but often over-stretched – staff, far outnumbered by dedicated volunteers. Let's start with the big three – The Royal Parks, City of London Corporation and Lee Valley Regional Park Authority. Then there are all the borough councils and other public bodies like the London Legacy Development Corporation which manages the Queen Elizabeth Olympic Park in Stratford. Helping to look after all of this are commercial grounds maintenance contractors like idverde UK, Glendale Services or SGM Commercial. On another tier, you'll find Parks for London, working with landowners and park managers. London Gardens Trust maintains a historic record of parks, squares, cemeteries, churchyards and community gardens, and scrutinises planning applications affecting public green space. The London Friends of Green Spaces Network brings together representatives from all the voluntary groups of different parks. In addition, many nature conservation organisations undertake specific works and activities in London's parks, such as guided walks, habitat restoration, wildlife monitoring or providing advice on biodiversity for park managers. Finally, there is the work of many partnerships to share best practice and help shape direct resource allocation.

Public attitudes towards parks have been transformed by the Covid-19 pandemic, with many people coming to rely on their local green spaces for exercise or as the only places they could socialise. They joined the dog walkers, families with young children and nature lovers who were already familiar with the parks' appeal.

This could easily lead to zoned areas of parks being set aside for different activities. We should expect investment in parks to ensure they are always there and able to support us through any future emergencies. Investment should also enable the parks themselves to add value to our landscape through water storage, energy generation or climate control.

Wildlife does not follow borders, so the artificial boundaries we place around our management and care of parks needs to reflect this. We need crossover between councils and organisations to ensure that habitats link up and that no one is reinventing the wheel. A good example of this is the collaboration that has created GoParksLondon, which aims to promote London's parks. Its website (see References & resources, page 190) includes an interactive online map focusing on the capital's more than four thousand parks and green spaces and offering information from a variety of partners involved in the sector.

New parks will be created in areas lacking green space, and some of these may well be on rooftops. A new development at Blackfriars is already creating a 0.4-hectare (1.1-acre) rooftop forest. Roots in the Sky will see the former Blackfriars Crown Court transformed into workspaces that have a community garden and a swimming pool on the roof, along with 1,300 tonnes of soil supporting 100 trees and 10,000 plants. Parklets and pocket parks will sprout up in streets where cars used to dominate.

Smart parks, which someone will no doubt dub iParks, are in the pipeline, with technology creeping into unexpected aspects of management and enjoyment. Look out for free wi-fi, charging points, and smart lighting that shines red at night to reduce light pollution but fades to white when people approach. QR codes offer online links to info on trees, historic monuments or nearby services and transport connections – or this will be provided using enhanced virtual reality. Park management will be made easier using a range of sensors to monitor moisture levels or light intensity, and smart bins will send an alert when they need emptying. We may even start listening to the plants in our parks now that we know they communicate chemically, electrically or via microbes.

Parks have been dramatically improved for wildlife – and people – in the past 30 years, but much more can be done if we are to help address the climate and nature crises. As the 19th-century, writer, poet and artist John Ruskin said, 'The measure of any great civilisation is its cities and a measure of a city's greatness is to be found in the quality of its public spaces, its parks and squares.' Today, I say bring it on. We can be the greatest and can inspire others to make the world greener, healthier and wilder.

PARKLET AT OSBORNE CLOSE

**STAG BEETLES** *Appearing briefly from May to July, these giants of the insect world may be found on Wimbledon and Putney Commons, in Epping Forest and in Richmond Park. They have been recorded in most boroughs, but you are more likely to spot one in a broad sweep from Bexle and Bromley in the sough-east, through to Hillingdon in the west.*

**DAFFODILS** *These are traditionally some of the earliest flowers to appear in most parks. Bunhill Fields burial ground off Moorgate is a great spot for daff watching. The Royal Parks plant a million daffodil bulbs across their parks every year. Others to check include Golders Hill Park in Golders Green, Springfield Park in Clapton, and Kew Gardens.*

**BIG BIRDS** *There are the clipped pelicans in St James's Park, but the capital has plenty of other big birds to spot. Regent's and Battersea Parks have healthy heronries, and Woodberry Wetlands has a good number of herons, too. You will probably find lone herons along many of the Thames tributaries where they pass through parks, including the Rivers Ingrebourne, Lee, Brent, Crane, Wandle, Ravensbourne and Cray, as well as along parts of the Thames, especially around Richmond upon Thames. Bitterns have been recorded in the reedbeds of the Lee Valley. Green Park has resident tawny owls – the tawny owl is London's most common owl, followed by little owl and then, much more rarely, barn owl.*

## NOTES

# Chapter 5 BY IAN HOLT

# LONDON'S HEATHLANDS

# A UNIQUE LANDSCAPE

It's a hot day and a steep climb through towering oak standards and old sweet chestnut coppice. We are heading up from the dark shade of a wooded valley and making for the light glimpsed briefly from beyond the forest canopy. The path we are following, sunk into the hillside, has been worn down slowly over centuries, most likely millennia. We pause for a moment just before reaching the brow of the hill, allowing some of our group to catch up and others to catch their breath. The next few steps are worth sharing, as the still air and dark greens of woodland in late summer are about to give way to something far more captivating. As we emerge from the cutting, our heads poke out level among a sea of purple heather spread across a plateau interspersed with gnarly, stunted and twisted oaks, the white and black trunks of birch, the automaton-like criss-cross hawking of dragonflies and the intense hum of countless foraging bees. The contrast with the woodland below could not be greater. We have arrived at Lesnes Heath.

Near Belvedere in the Borough of Bexley, Lesnes (or Lessness) Heath is a small remnant of lowland heath. A habitat that can vary greatly from place to place, heathland is generally characterised as being low in nutrients, often with free-draining acidic soils, areas of bare ground and patches of grass, and is dominated by shrubs such as heather, broom and gorse. Among this mosaic of microhabitats, acidic bogs with their highly specialised flora may also be found, but tree cover is sparse, creating an openness where the full force of the sun can be felt along with the lash of wind and rain.

Heaths are ancient and man-made landscapes, in areas of poor soil, where trees were removed over many centuries, and were unable to regrow because of grazing or burning. At Lesnes and other heathland or former heathland sites, including nearby Winn's Common in Plumstead and the more famous Hampstead Heath in north London, this link with the past can be witnessed through the presence of ancient burial mounds, or barrows. The Lesnes barrow, also referred to as a tumulus, in nearby Lesnes Abbey Wood (see page 161), has suffered from historical excavations, leaving the mound quartered and a little reminiscent of a giant hot cross bun; mountain biking has not helped the look either.

# ANCIENT
# COPPICED OAKS

Among the most iconic features of **Lesnes Heath** are the ancient coppiced oaks, which at first do not sound very characteristic of heathland at all. However, these trees, short in stature, bulbous and multistemmed, and each with its own distinctive character, indicate the impoverished soils typical of the habitat. This is especially notable when compared not just with the grand oaks of the adjoining woodland but also with the vigorous oaks of only 20–25 years of age that have begun to colonise the heath. The tall, straight trunks of these young trees may demonstrate the benefits of more recent nutrification caused by a build-up of organic plant matter, air pollution and dog fouling. Closer inspection of the coppiced trees reveals that they are of a different species to the oaks in the adjoining woods, which are predominantly pedunculate, or English, oaks *Quercus robur*. The coppiced trees are sessile oaks *Quercus petraea*, distinguishable by their stalked leaves and stalkless acorns. Being more drought-tolerant, these coppiced trees prefer light, well-drained, even rocky soil. Whether sessile oaks colonised the heath naturally or whether the Augustinian canons of Lesnes Abbey selected them for their ability to grow in such conditions we may never find out, but we do know that the trees were actively managed and harvested as a crop.

Colonisation by trees and increased nutrients are constant threats to this habitat and must be managed if the heath is to survive and its succession to woodland be prevented. These days the trees are managed by the pulling of saplings and selective felling, but not of the veteran trees and not too many at a time. The perception that all trees are good for the environment is deeply ingrained, and the subtleties of site management are not always appreciated by those alerted by the sound of chainsaws.

# SUPPORTING HEATHER AND OTHER WILDLIFE

Looking around this landscape you will see a number of mysterious pits, usually square and no more than 5cm (2in) deep. They have been dug to remove the top layer of nutrient-rich organic matter and expose the sandy gravel. This both exposes any existing heather seedbank and allows it to germinate free from the competition of more nutrient-loving plants. Occasionally the pits are triangular or round, although this is due to the boredom of digging pits rather than the propagation of common heather *Calluna vulgaris*.

The life cycle of heather is divided into four stages – pioneer, building, mature and degenerate. It is important to have a balance between each of these to maximise the heath's biodiversity. The young plants in the pioneer phase, looking like microscopic Christmas trees, are vulnerable to trampling. In the degenerate phase, the heather lies across the ground. If there is too much, it may suppress the seedlings.

The heather at Lesnes is common heather, also known as ling, but there are a few sites in London where you can see bell heather *Erica cinerea*, which likes dry ground, and cross-leaved heath *Erica tetralix* which prefers wetter areas such as the bogs on Wimbledon and Keston Commons. These sites are home to rare plants including bog asphodel *Narthecium ossifragum* and veilwort *Pallavicinia lyellii*. A visit to Keston Bog will see you following in the footsteps of Charles Darwin, who studied carnivorous sundew plants there.

Now fragmented, London's heaths cannot support many of the rarer wildlife species found on larger sites, but treasures are still there to be seen. Reptiles thrive in heathland, where the bare earth and dense shrubs give them perfect conditions for basking and hunting invertebrate prey. It was at Lesnes Heath over 25 years ago, while clearing oak saplings and bramble from the heather as a volunteer, that I first saw a London lizard. It was one of the moments that focused my mind towards a career in nature conservation and a return to Lesnes as Estate Manager decades later.

# MANAGING
# OUR HEATHLAND

The human activity that, through necessity, created and sustained our heaths for millennia has largely come to an end, and certainly this is the case in London. While in the 19th century the people of Plumstead and Woolwich rose up to protect their rights to graze livestock, cut turf and dig for aggregates on Plumstead Common, nobody is claiming the right to do so now. Ultimately, urban expansion and changing priorities for society and therefore land use have greatly diminished the quantity and quality of our heathland. In London an area of no more than 80 hectares (200 acres) of heathland still exists, and half of this is on **Wimbledon Common** and **Putney Heath**. This represents a dramatic decline in a city where numerous place names such as **Thornton Heath** (in south London), **Chadwell Heath** (near Romford) and **Northumberland Heath** (near Erith) confirm the former extent of this habitat in the wider landscape. How many people living in or visiting the city today make the connection between heathland and **Heathrow**? Or know that the iconic heathland bird the **Dartford warbler**, or furze wren as it is also known, was first recorded not on **Dartford Heath** but in **Bexleyheath**? Alas, the only furze wren to be found in Bexleyheath now is a pub.

London's experience mirrors that of Britain as a whole. It is estimated that only about 16 per cent of the habitat that existed in 1800 remains. However, that 16 per cent is believed to be 20 per cent of all heathland globally. Given this backdrop, the survival of any heath in London is to be celebrated, not only for its ecological importance but for its historical and cultural significance, too.

# **Gorse and broom:** scents of coconut and vanilla

Common gorse *Ulex europaeus* and common broom *Cytisus scoparius* are two iconic heathland shrubs with attractive yellow flowers and magical scents. Both members of the pea family, they have similar strategies for survival but their own distinct cultural histories.

Gorse and broom share an ability to fix nitrogen through a symbiotic relationship with bacteria that live in special nodules on the plant's roots. The bacteria convert nitrogen from the atmosphere, which the plants cannot use, into a form they can exploit for plant growth and essential functions such as photosynthesis. This ability to fix nitrogen in impoverished heathland soils gives broom and gorse a competitive advantage over plants without this capability.

Both species flower profusely to attract pollinators including honeybees and bumblebees. Broom flowers from April to July and produces a vanilla scent. Gorse tends to flower from January to June but can flower at other times throughout the year as well. This, along with the fact that two closely related species, dwarf gorse and Western gorse, flower later, probably gave rise to the old saying, 'When gorse is out of bloom, kissing is out of fashion'.

On a hot day these flowers can fill the air with a wonderfully intense and exotic smell of coconut.

In 1736 the Swedish naturalist Carl Linnaeus is reputed to have fallen to his knees and praised God for the beautiful display of flowering gorse bushes he encountered while crossing Putney Heath. Not to be outdone, broom, known in medieval times as *Planta genista*, is thought to have given its name to the Plantagenet dynasty of kings, who wore a sprig of broom as their emblem.

Seed dispersal is also similar between the two species, which use exploding pods to fling the next generation off and away from the parent. On a hot and sunny day, moisture in the pods dries up, causing tension within the pod which splits violently and audibly. The sound can be disconcertingly reminiscent of a crackling wildfire. In fact, gorse and broom are highly flammable and their seeds germinate well after fires which kill off competing plants. Broom and gorse are also believed to benefit from seed dispersal by ants. Their seeds have attached to them something called an elaiosome, a structure containing fats and proteins that attracts the ants which then carry the seed back to the nest before eating the elaiosome and discarding the seed.

Despite their similarities, gorse and broom are easy to tell apart. Broom is a deciduous shrub with small, trifoliate leaves, while the leaves of the evergreen gorse are modified to create a mass of sharp green spines. These modified leaves not only help protect the plant from grazing but also reduce water loss. Bird species such as Dartford warbler and whinchat also benefit from the protection provided by the spines of gorse, among which they will readily hide or nest, although unfortunately not in London. The whin of whinchat, like furze, is another common name for gorse.

The long and flexible branches of broom are naturally bundled closely together, making it ideal for sweeping, and it was traditionally used to do so, hence the name. Other uses for broom include eating (broom buds), brewing, thatching, tanning and dyeing. Gorse has far fewer traditional uses than broom, but one of them was as a winter feed for livestock. The branches would be milled to crush the spines, so that it was more palatable. Its combustibility made it a popular source as fuel.

# NOTES

# Chapter 6
BY DANIEL GREENWOOD

# AUTUMN IN LONDON'S WOODLANDS

Imagine a mild October morning: autumn is building in London's Great North Wood, an ancient landscape of woods and commons that once stretched from Croydon to near the Thames at Deptford. In Sydenham Hill Wood, one of the largest remaining remnants, there are the first hints of yellow in the hornbeam leaves, a seasonal staple of this London clay-based landscape. Hundreds of people will visit here today: families getting much needed outdoor time after a long week, Sunday walkers completing a section of the Green Chain Walk, and volunteers going to and from their meeting point for a day's toil in support of vital conservation efforts.

Though we are focused on the leaves falling from the trees above us at this time of year, something is pushing up from the ground below: mushrooms. If you look around you at the mature trees towering overhead and consider the soil covered by the summer's growths of wildflowers, you will see the work of the fungal kingdom. While we thank trees for all they do for us, for the habitats they provide for wildlife and the shelter of their canopies, it's not the whole story. Without the work of fungi in both feeding trees and recycling them into soil, there would be no woods at all.

# WELCOME TO THE 'WOOD WIDE WEB'

We are able to walk through woodland without meeting a mountain of fallen trees and other organic material because the circle of life is well and truly established in this landscape. Fungi have been at work for many millions of years on earth, at times maintaining rich supplies of nutrients and minerals to trees that they are unable to acquire alone. Our freedom to pass through the landscape is because of the breaking up of woody material that a landscape produces year on year. As a visitor to one of London's fragile woods, you have stumbled into the ancient underground social network recently dubbed the 'Wood Wide Web'.

A natural response to seeing a tree that has fallen is sadness at the loss of a friend. Perhaps this is a tree you have known since childhood, that you have sat underneath at times of sadness or hardship. It has given you not just oxygen to breathe, but space and a sense of belonging. The affection we have for trees can sometimes stop us from appreciating the true picture of nature. The tree so close to your heart has almost certainly developed local friendships of its own, with the underground webs of fungi providing it with sustenance over many years. Its root hairs have connected with the networks of microscopic fungal hyphae (filament structures) in the soil, passing water, nutrients and minerals in

a manner not unlike the passage of data in a broadband connection.

Walking in October in a woodland where trees have been allowed to fall and remain intact will reveal many deadwood-loving mushrooms. Common species such as sulphur tuft grow in profusion on fallen trees but also in the soil, sometimes attached to woody debris just below the surface. Honey fungus, a species many gardeners fear for its ability to withhold nutrients to some trees, causing their decline, explodes onto the scene at this time of year. Around the log and brush piles made by volunteers as habitat, you will find turkey tail, hairy curtain crust and inkcap vying for the new resources brought about by this decaying matter. These microhabitats also provide nooks and crannies for beautiful slime moulds to appear, a group of organisms that are not actually fungi and may be more closely related to the animal kingdom.

Check the damaged branches of an elder tree and you will find jelly ear, which looks exactly like its name. On ash wood you can discover King Alfred's cakes, a fungus that looks like lumps of coal, named after the story of the exiled king's failure to keep an eye on a peasant baker's dozen.

If you think about it, the role of fungi in sustaining London's woods and trees means the city itself has mushrooms to thank for its development. Though London is now largely a city of tarmac, brick, glass and concrete, its early beginnings involved timber-framed buildings made from oak and elm. The fires that fuelled the blacksmiths' forges, bakers' ovens and domestic hearths of old London were based on charcoal produced in woods around the city's fringes, with hornbeam one of the most important fuels for London's colliers.

Hornbeam is not a common tree but some of London's ancient woodlands are key reservoirs for this member of the birch family. It lives on clay and has rock-solid timber and muscular bark. Each year it produces ornate seed cases that fall not far

TOP ROW: FLY AGARIC; FUNGI AT SYDENHAM HILL WOOD; COMMON FUNNEL CAP BOTTOM ROW: LICHEN AND MOSS; TURKEY TAIL; HORNBEAM LEAVES

from the tree, meaning hornbeam does not spread far and can maintain strongholds in groves of its own. Once known as 'hardbeam', it is renowned for its toughness, despite the elegant seed dispersal and the subtle beauty of its leaves. Looking up at those leaves appearing in spring gives the sense of being underwater, with the leaves floating on the surface above.

# From acorns to oaks

As autumn draws to a close, and the bare branches of trees are stark against wintry skies, we sometimes find ourselves at the tail end of a mast year for London's acorns. Mast is another name for nuts or seeds, with beech nuts often referred to as 'beech-mast'. A mast year is when the weather and temperatures in spring and summer have created the right conditions for a bumper crop.

Oaks are wind-pollinated, one of nature's first reproductive mechanisms for plants. It is thought to have evolved with the arrival of spore-bearing mosses hundreds of millions of years ago. Trees like cherry and others in the rose family are pollinated by bees, butterflies, moths and flies.

Though cherries are far tastier than acorns, the oak's fruit is one of the most important to us for several reasons. When acorns fall into leaf litter, many of them will not be broken down by fungi. Instead, jays will 'cache' acorns, planting thousands of them to feed themselves over the winter. Grey squirrels do exactly the same.

In Britain the hazelnut has been one of the single most important food sources for people, especially before farming when hunter-gatherers relied on wild diets. Archaeologists have found regular evidence of hazelnut shells at prehistoric settlement sites, sometimes in vast numbers. There is also evidence that our hunter-gatherers cooked hazel into a paste that could be taken on long journeys. It's the very definition of fast food.

# So galling

One of the most fascinating cultural impacts of the acorn is when it is missing and is replaced by a parasite. In the spring, tiny parasitic wasps appear from galls (a gall is a growth that has prospered in the place of an acorn) and each lays its own eggs in an acorn bud. A chemical reaction takes place in the tissue of the plant and a gall is formed.

There are many species of gall, and a lot of them are not instigated by solitary wasps, but one of the most significant for human civilisation has been the oak apple gall. It was imported into Britain over a thousand years ago for its prime use in the creation of ink. The galls can be ground down and mixed with chemicals to make a black ink. It was this ink that was used to write almost all of the major doctrines and political agreements in the western world, including the Magna Carta and the American Declaration of Independence. That sylvan scripture known as the Charter of the Forest of 1217, re-establishing the common man's right of access to forests, will also have been transcribed in oak gall ink. Amazingly, it was only in the 1970s that the German government stopped using oak gall ink for use in all official documentation!

# Sci-fi wasps

Wasps are much-maligned creatures in Britain but there are many different species found in London's woods. Though we are well acquainted with the common social wasps that bother people at picnics when the wasps are in their 'sugar-lust' phase, there are thousands of other species. In woodlands where a reasonable amount of decaying wood can be found, ichneumon wasps are seeking to complete, to us perhaps, one of nature's most unpleasant ecological processes.

A female ichneumon use her needlelike ovipositor to 'inject' her eggs into the burrows of insects, crevices in wood or, most appallingly to the human mind, the larvae of other insects. The ichneumon's eggs hatch inside the live caterpillar and eat it. It was probably the inspiration for some science fiction films (but to balance things out, insects inspired the creation of Pokémon!).

Britain is not blessed with the same species diversity as many other countries, but there are over two thousand species of ichneumon wasp. Though their ecology is grisly, like almost all of the most misunderstood insects, they are pollinators of plants, crops and flowers. Wasps are also key pest controllers in both wild habitats and agricultural landscapes. We really need to understand them better and up our conservation game to protect these crucial animals.

In the insect world, it's not just wasps that depend on London's woodlands to survive. One rare species is famous for its preference for city life.

# Stag party

For anyone growing up in London, the sight of a stag beetle on the pavement is probably not unusual. You can see where insects get the name 'mini-beasts' when you look at this creature: its huge mandibles give it a sense of outward aggression, as if it's constantly spoiling for a fight. The reality is different, unless you're another male stag beetle, which may be wrestled to submission.

When you witness a stag beetle flying around, the impression is of an animal that's not quite with it. But stag beetles are perfectly harmless and have, like much of Britain's wildlife, suffered immense declines since the 1940s. Like ichneumon wasps and their prey, stag beetles are dependent on rotting wood in woodland habitats.

The suburban sprawl of the post-war period saw extensive loss of habitat in Britain. Ancient woods were felled and grubbed out, and the wider countryside tidy-up has been very damaging to wildlife like stag beetles. Strangely enough, for reasons not fully understood, London is still a good place to find these insects, particularly across much of south and outer western London.

This almost cartoon-like beetle can be seen on calm evenings between May and July, at a time when bats are often most active. If you set yourself up in a clearing in a south London woodland during this time, you may encounter a stag beetle and pipistrelle bat flying in close proximity as they go about their business. The champion flyer out of those two species is quite clearly the bat.

One of the most interesting aspects of a stag beetle's lifestyle is also bittersweet. The adult beetle we sometimes see is only in existence for four to six weeks. In the insect's larval stage, it can live underground for as long as six years, where it spends its time working its way through decaying wood lodged underground, aided by fungi's powers of decay. It's warm down there, so the seasons aren't an issue for London's subterranean stag beetle grubs.

# The great spotted wood striker

Grubs are top of the menu for one of London's most iconic bird species. A standing or fallen dead tree with large holes excavated from its rotting trunk is testament to how tasty it finds these larvae. But this bird is best-known for its noisy antics in the treetops – the rattling in the canopies of woods, parks and gardens stops many in their tracks. It's a sound that brings in the new year, the first signs of spring breaking through as our own seasonal celebrations draw to an end. While we are still deep into indulging our need to rest in the midwinter, this bird is busy setting out on its quest for new life. It is the great spotted woodpecker.

Britain is home to three species of woodpecker, but in January the hammering, or drumming, we begin to hear is that of the great spotted – the males are marking new territories. It's a bird that is becoming more and more familiar to Londoners as its numbers increase.

Its favoured habitat is oak woodland, with plenty of rotting branches, trunks and limbs in which to create a new hole each year. This is an ample habitat for the great spotted, which is the biggest of our two 'spotted' woodpeckers (also known as

Dendrocopos which translates from Greek as 'wood-striker'.)

One thing you may have noticed in suburban locations is the woodpecker drumming on TV aerials and receivers. Some woodpeckers have found that the plastic box now employed to improve TV signals makes decent percussion. It's a wonder that this hammering on hard surfaces doesn't cause the birds injury, but evolution has equipped them with shock absorbers in the back of their skulls that cushion the blow. It's not the same as banging your head against the wall.

There are four members of the woodpecker family native to Britain, but one – the wryneck – is now classified as extinct as a breeding bird. The wryneck still migrates from Africa each spring in small numbers. In 1904 one nested in what was thought by the observer to be one of the last nests in his time in southeast London.

Another of our four species has declined at a rate that has baffled ornithologists. The lesser spotted woodpecker was noted breeding in London's woods up until 2012. Small numbers of lesser spotted are still recorded as it is migratory.

Green woodpeckers are different from the spotted woodpeckers because they don't hammer to mark their territories. Instead, they call, which was known for centuries as 'yaffling' – an old name for a green woodpecker is 'yaffler'. It's a call that can be heard most clearly in woods and parks with mature trees, where they nest. The call has a prehistoric feel about it, echoing deep into woodland and giving a sense of wilderness as the reverberation melts away.

Greens also differ from the spotted woodpeckers because of their feeding habits, spending their time searching for ant colonies in woods and lawns. Naturally grassy sports pitches with a surrounding area of mature trees are a good place to find the birds. They lie low, shooting their long tongues down into ants' nests to find food. It's something you are very unlikely ever to see a great spotted woodpecker do.

# NOTES

_____

_____

_____

_____

_____

_____

_____

_____

_____

_____

_____

_____

_____

# Chapter 7  BY KABIR KAUL

# WETLANDS & RESERVOIRS

# A VISIT ON A WINTER'S MORNING

Our capital's wetlands and waterbodies are scattered across the suburbs, and each one has a story. From ancient, extensive marshes on the banks of the Thames to reservoirs and gravel pits, these blue jewels in London's ecological crown have become important havens for wildlife, especially waterbirds.

It's a cold, crisp winter's morning at my local wetland, a former reservoir. Dark, ominous clouds dominate the sky, but nevertheless the residents begin to wake up. The majestic male **mute swan** is the first to make a sound, grunting with effort and arrogantly trying to present his huge wingspan to his sleeping family. They, too, wake up and all of them swim to shore, with a cacophony of unpleasant grunting and snorting. The texture of this noise is thickened when the swans are joined by **Canada geese**, a familiar sight on our waterbodies. They eagerly assemble near the fence that separates the water from managed parkland, with the knowledge that a feast will soon be provided for them by human visitors.

The waves are choppy, almost violent, tossing smaller wildfowl about like toys. This wakes a flock of sleeping **mallards**, the quintessential British duck. The males have distinct green heads, in contrast to the females, which, like most female ducks, have feathers of different shades of brown. Both sexes have striking Prussian-blue secondary feathers on their wings. They all raise their heads in utter confusion, before taking to the air with a chorus of quacking. The most numerous duck on the water, the **tufted duck**, is unaffected by the temperamental waves. Unlike the mallard, which gingerly sticks its head into the water to feed, the 'tuftie' dives confidently beneath the waves. These gorgeous ducks can be easily identified by their blue bills, and the eponymous tuft at the back of their heads.

Meanwhile, in the safety and shelter of the overhanging trees, winter migrants are waking from their slumber. Sizeable flocks of **shovelers** and **pochards** have migrated here on a remarkable journey, to escape the cold winters in northern Europe and feed at the lake. These two birds add splashes of colour to the otherwise bleak winter landscape. The heads of male pochards are a reddish-brown colour, while those of male shovelers are green, and their bill gives the species its name: I once read that a shoveler feeds 'as if it's lost its contact lenses'. These shy migrant ducks take their time to venture out into the water, a sea of orange and green that eventually disperses into small groups.

On the very edge of the lake, a pair of **Egyptian geese** sit near a grass verge. These geese are descendants of captive birds that had escaped into the wild, and are smaller than Canada geese. The brown and beige hues of their feathers help them to blend in well with the vast, concrete edges of the former reservoir, and they merely look at the bustling lake, choosing not to be part of the excitement themselves.

Amid this colossal gathering of wildfowl, other residents are beginning their day. A **moorhen** utters a watery 'pur' and squeaks like a rubber duck, while trying to travel through the masses of mallards that are heading to shore: a panicked commuter caught in the middle of rush hour. Its beak looks as if the bird had dipped it in red and yellow paint, unlike its cousin the

TOP ROW: EGYPTIAN GOOSE; MALE POCHARD; SHOVELER DUCK
BOTTOM ROW: LITTLE RINGED PLOVER; TUFTED DUCK; FIELDFARE

coot, which has other impressive features. Choosing to stay away from the crowd, the **coot** is a much larger, bulkier bird than the moorhen. Its beak is a brilliant white, but it is only when the bird walks on land that I appreciate it entirely: its large, blue, dinosaur-like feet will surprise any passer-by.

I notice that there is, of course, another dominant family of birds in the water, the **gulls**. They are not everyone's cup of tea, stealing people's chips at the seaside and frequently being raucous. I scan them with my binoculars, and most appear to be black-headed gulls, the UK's most common species. They can be recognised by their all-black head in summer, but in winter they have a black spot below their eye. Some of them take to the air, looking for scraps of food nearby, while others sit calmly on the water, moving with the turbulent waves. In contrast, some of the larger gulls, possibly **common** or **lesser black-backed gulls**, find themselves more comfortable closer to shore among the Canada geese and mute swans.

The final participant in this gathering of waterbirds is unlike any other. The **great crested grebe**, almost extinct in London a hundred years ago, is now a common sight across our urban wetlands and reservoirs. They exhibit their full splendour in spring, when their iconic mating dance can be seen: the birds will shake their heads for over an hour, then offer weeds and leap at each other with determination. Their most distinct feature is the red and orange 'mane' of feathers surrounding their heads. During the winter months, grebes shed these feathers and look somewhat less charismatic. At my local wetland, winter is coming to an end, so the birds have become rather shy and solitary. I have difficulty finding them, as they tend to spend most of their time diving to catch fish and find weeds.

Away from the water itself, other avian inhabitants prefer to perch in the nearby trees, logs and bushes. I raise my binoculars, and with difficulty attempt to look beyond the breadth of the waterbody. There, like a motionless statue on a fallen tree, a **grey heron** looks eagerly down into the water. By its side are a dozen **cormorants**, surrounding it like loyal attendants, all examining the water on a search for their breakfast. This staring contest with the waves continues for 15 minutes, but nothing happens. With the exception of the heron and the cormorants, the marshy areas near the former reservoir are silent, longing for the vibrant songs of **Cetti's** and **reed warblers**, which will return on their migration from Africa in the spring.

The sky above is quiet, too, apart from a **buzzard**, a tiny speck in the sky. In July and August, migratory **swifts, swallows** and **house martins** dart above the lake, feeding on insects with an ecstasy of screeching. Some build their nests and breed in the eaves of nearby houses, but these works of art lie almost untouched during this cold winter morning. Occasionally, a wading bird like a **dunlin, little ringed plover** or **green sandpiper** makes its way to the wetland. None are here this morning, but wading birds are common on most of London's wetlands and reservoirs.

The adjacent parkland, where people picnic and play football in summer, is alive with activity. I find it important not just to appreciate the rare birds I have witnessed in the past, but to find joy in seeing the common, everyday birds too. The sweet song of the **robin** fills my ears as I look up into the tangled maze of branches. A **blackbird** joins in and is quickly complemented by a charm of **goldfinches**. The latter have beautiful red, black and yellow plumage, and the timbre of

their song sounds similar to the jangling of keys. Then a movement within my peripheral vision sends my binoculars pointing to the skies. A flock of **redwings** and **fieldfares**, uttering a high-pitched 'tseep-tseep', moves hurriedly over the parkland. These are not ordinary thrushes, but winter visitors – like the shovelers and pochards, they have migrated from northern Europe, excited to guzzle berries on bushes in our parks and gardens.

Briefly, my curiosity returns to the ground, as I've heard a panicked 'chissick' noise on the grass. Three **pied wagtails** are moving around on the ground, wagging their tails up and down and drinking from the water. This race of the white wagtail is one of three wagtails found here, with the other two commonly seen around the lake in summer. **Wood pigeons** add a dissonance to the melodious birdsong, lamenting with their guttural cooing; its rhythm is popularly memorised through the words 'my-toe-is-blee-ding'. The melancholy call is soon drowned out

by the last participant in this eventful song. A myriad of metallic-sounding flight calls pass over my head, and I know that this is yet again a winter visitor. The **lesser redpoll** has been recently recognised as a separate species from the larger common redpoll and is a member of the finch family. Ten of them swarm to the tops of trees overhanging the lake, begin to feed noisily and then move back into the nearby meadows and woods.

The elaborate show ends and the songbirds begin to start their day. Each waterbody in London is unique, and though it may not seem obvious at first, nature has found a way to flourish and adapt in all of them. London's wildlife is hiding in plain sight, and through our wetlands and reservoirs, we can each find a way to connect with it.

# THE DEVELOPMENT OF LONDON'S WETLANDS & RESERVOIRS

If you look at a map of London, you will see noticeable areas of blue, and, in fact, two per cent of London is currently considered 'blue space', which includes wetlands, reservoirs and rivers. However, our reservoir habitats have been created relatively recently. Until the 19th century, the population of the city had relied on springs and local watercourses for drinking water. But from the 1830s, a number of water companies started to build reservoirs on the outskirts of the then city for this purpose. Others had been constructed earlier to provide water for the emerging network of canals, which were used to transport goods.

Over the next hundred years, the reservoirs built to feed canals were gradually converted into recreational facilities. By the 1970s, most of the capital's Victorian reservoirs were still being used to supply drinking water to Greater London, and new waterbodies were created through the extraction of gravel. However, the importance of London's reservoirs to wildlife was starting to be recognised. Several were given special status, protecting the waterbirds that lived there. Today, most of them, some still supplying Londoners with their daily drinking water, continue to be managed to protect the capital's biodiversity.

Meanwhile, London's wetlands have a different story. Most of the low-lying wetlands along the capital's rivers have been artificially created, or maintained in various ways over the centuries, so there are few examples of naturally occurring wetlands left. In Medieval times, much of modern-day London alongside rivers consisted of marshes. Over the centuries most of this habitat was drained to be farmed, before eventually built upon. Remnants of these ancient marshes can be found on the banks of the Thames, and some parts have been almost untouched since they were used by passing livestock for grazing centuries ago: Rainham Marshes, on the edge of Havering, is a good example. Although most wetland habitats in their current guise are relatively young, they, like our reservoirs, support a wealth of wildlife.

# A FEW OF THE BEST WETLANDS & RESERVOIRS THAT CAN BE EXPLORED IN LONDON

## Colne Valley Regional Park
### Hillingdon

Spanning the extreme western fringes of Greater London, the park straddles five counties. London's portion of the park – 117 hectares (289 acres) – contains huge **former gravel pits**, which are regionally important for **wildfowl, water vole, otter** and populations of **rare bats**, as well as **wet meadow** and **ancient woodland**. The rivers that flow through the Colne Valley have created an extensive area of **wetlands**, several of which are managed as nature reserves.

## Rainham Marshes
### Havering/Thurrock

Once a shooting range owned by the Ministry of Defence, the RSPB's nature reserve on the London/Esses borders – 411 hectares (1,016 acres) – is one of the best birding sites in the capital. Situated on the Thames Estuary, the **ancient marshes** include **reedbeds, scrubland** and **saltmarshes**, providing a home for **birds, lizards, frogs** and **dragonflies**. It has an excellent visitor centre and many paths to explore, perfect for a family day out.

# Lee Valley Regional Park
## Enfield, Waltham Forest, Haringey, Hackney, Tower Hamlets and Newham

From Hertfordshire, this 42km- (26 mile-) long broad valley –
946 hectares (2,337 acres) of it – stretches down to Bow Creek in
Docklands. From working reservoirs to former dockyards, it includes
the Queen Elizabeth Olympic Park and Europe's largest urban
wetland, Walthamstow Wetlands. All of these wetland habitats,
and the rivers and creeks between them, support a vast array of
biodiversity, including **water vole, otter,** fish and internationally
important populations of some birds.

# London Wetland Centre
## Barnes, Richmond-upon-Thames

These former reservoirs beside the Thames – 40 hectares (99 acres)
– are now a thriving wetland habitat in southwest London. The
founder of the Wildfowl & Wetlands Trust (WWT), Sir Peter Scott,
wished to see a wetland in London similar to that at his home in
Slimbridge, Gloucestershire. The result of his vision was established
in 2000: there now are plenty of reedbeds and lakes, supporting
hundreds of **wintering waterbirds,** including the nationally rare
**bittern.** There are multi-levelled hides and a restaurant, so one can
watch urban wildlife in comfort.

# Woodberry Wetlands
## Hackney

Still a working drinking water reservoir in Hackney, closed to the
public for almost 200 years, this calm oasis is also a beautiful urban
wetland nature reserve. Opened by Sir David Attenborough in 2016
it is a thriving habitat for migratory birds, such **reed warblers** from
west Africa, and resident species including the **kingfisher** and **great
crested grebe.** Hedgerows and wildflowers line the banks of the
reservoir, while islands provide a wetland haven for waterfowl. The
lovely café makes this a much loved visitor attraction.

# Common kingfisher: a flash of turquoise and gold

**On any day of the year, along most of London's waterways and reservoirs, it is quite possible that a fast flash of gold and blue will be seen over the water. The common kingfisher *Alcedo atthis* is one of our most iconic waterbirds, and an iridescent jewel in our lakes, streams and rivers. It is found throughout the UK, with the exception of upland habitats and northern Scotland, and is fairly common across London.**

Britain's breeding kingfishers are a subspecies (*Alcedo atthis ispida*) that has lived in the country for many thousands of years, with the oldest fossil specimens dating from around 120,000 years ago. They are unmistakable, easily identified by their magnificent metallic blue back and wings, and bright orange underparts. A distinguishing feature between males and females is the beak colour: males have all-black beaks, while those of females have a red base. Kingfishers do not sing, but their call is a sharp, repeated 'chee-kee' or 'chreee'; this is often heard beneath the vegetation of a riverbank.

When feeding, the birds will first find a perch to sit on over the water. This is usually a tree branch, but some have used discarded shopping trolleys on occasions. Motionless,

they will wait for small fish to swim past, then hover and dive headfirst into the water. Once a kingfisher has caught its prey, it will repeatedly beat the head of the fish on a branch until it is stunned, before swallowing it whole. A varied diet is enjoyed by the birds, feeding on loach, minnow, stickleback and the occasional mayfly in spring.

From February to March, kingfishers will begin to mate, secure territories and excavate their nests in riverbanks. According to the ancient Greek philosopher Aristotle, the birds would build their nests during the winter solstice, and the gods would calm the Mediterranean Sea during this period. Because the kingfisher's other name is the halcyon, this time of the year became known as the 'halcyon days' and the term is now used when referring to calm weather during this period, or simple days of peace. Coincidentally, some of the British population do migrate from the Mediterranean to breed here. Birds will lay their eggs in April, and London's kingfishers sometimes do this in holes in walls near waterbodies, showing that they have adapted well to our concrete jungle.

Five to seven eggs are usually laid by the parents. The young will rely on them for the next 27 days, until they are driven out,

so that the adults can attempt to breed once more in a year. The fledglings will have a life span of two years, but unfortunately fewer are surviving to adulthood. In addition to cold winters, which can kill dozens of birds when waterbodies freeze over, the capital's population is vulnerable to water pollution. Since 1970, kingfishers in London's wetlands and reservoirs have suffered greatly due to a build-up in plastic waste. As they are high up in the food chain, the birds are frequently poisoned through bioaccumulation, with chemicals and plastic particles being ingested through the fish they eat. Chemicals and sewage severely affect fish populations, too, so kingfishers will tend to move elsewhere if they cannot find food easily.

However, there is hope for the kingfishers in our urban wetlands and waterways. Organisations and volunteers across most of the capital are helping to clean up and restore the river tributaries of the Thames. This will ensure that biodiversity, including fish populations, can flourish in these areas once more, providing these stunning birds with a much-needed food supply. With this, let us hope that the halcyon days for London's kingfishers will arrive soon enough.

# Eurasian teal: small, shy and agile

During winter, countless numbers of ducks leave their freezing, Nordic breeding grounds and migrate south to Britain. Among this hardy family of birds is the Eurasian teal *Anas crecca*, which decides to spend these rather cold months in inland reservoirs, lakes and coastal lagoons. Their wintering population is unevenly distributed across Britain, with migratory birds arriving in London and the southwest of England; coastal areas of Scotland; the west of Wales; and a significant portion of Northern Ireland. While there is a sizeable visiting population, a lot of teals reside all year round in the Britain's wetlands.

Our resident teals were first recorded in medieval times, and today their population numbers around 3,700 breeding pairs. As with most other species of duck, the males are the stars of the show; the television presenter and past-President of the RSPB, Kate Humble, once referred to them as 'the Ziggy Stardust of the duck world'. Despite sometimes being a shy duck, the male definitely stands out with its russet head and noticeable green stripe down its eye, as well as the mesmerising patterns below its wings. Meanwhile, the female has brown plumage, also with beautiful patterns, complemented with a flash of bright green beneath its wing. In summer, the gorgeous male will moult: in this 'eclipse' plumage, it will almost resemble the female and will be unable to fly for a month.

Males and females have different calls, with the male's being a flutey 'krit krit'. This inspired the Swedish name for the bird, crecca, now used as part of its scientific name, and surprisingly, the bird has not been known by any other name besides 'teal'. The female's call is rather different, being a high-pitched quacking.

The collective noun for the birds is a 'spring', referring to the way they take off from the water vertically; despite their unsteady gait on land, the birds can reach a top speed of 80kph (50mph) in the air. Teals will frequently be observed in flocks, and their feeding habits are unique: inactive during the day with regard to feeding, the birds will dabble around their wetland habitat, searching for grasses, rush seeds and pondweed. This changes dramatically in summer, when resident birds will eat water snails, fly larvae and aquatic worms for a meal. Birds have a specialised filtration system when feeding, with tooth-like ridges called lamellae, acting as sieves. From October to November, migratory birds from mainland Europe arrive, which significantly increases our teal population;

around this time, resident birds will start finding mates and nesting sites. It is only after the migratory birds have left, in April, that the female will lay eight to eleven eggs. Because London has an abundance of waterbodies, many of them managed to benefit waterbirds, there is plenty of space for teals to nest in our urban wetlands and reservoirs.

During the 21-day incubation, the brightly coloured male will desert the nest, leaving the female to raise the ducklings. After 30 days, the ducklings will become independent, and able to breed around their first birthday. The oldest teal recorded was a remarkable 21 years old.

Unlike most population trends of ducks, teal numbers in the Britain are increasing. The birds' upland habitat has been threatened by the planting of commercial forests in the past, but now the teal is protected during the breeding season. Historically, they were regarded as a delicacy and in the 17th century were used for medicinal purposes, as 'duck grease'; fortunately no longer a threat to them. However, birds are potentially vulnerable to pollution in our urban wetlands, as they could accidentally ingest small parts of litter or plastic through their sophisticated feeding systems. Urban predators like foxes occasionally feed on their eggs, and a similar problem occurs with introduced American mink in other parts of the country. Despite these threats, the work of London's conservation charities has helped to establish a vast array of rich wetland ecosystems in the capital, providing the perfect habitat for both resident and migratory teals. It seems that for the foreseeable future, these vibrant ducks will remain a much-loved part of our capital's waterbodies.

## NOTES

# Chapter 8  BY ANNA GUERIN
# LONDON'S GRASSLANDS

# A SUMMER'S DAY
# IN A MEADOW

A meadow in summertime
– sun shining, bees buzzing,
grass swishing – may remind
many of a rural childhood or a
countryside idyll, reached only
after a long journey during
the school holidays, but for
Londoners this experience may
be much closer than they think.
Thanks to the chalky soils of the
London Basin slicing through
the capital, pockets of chalk
grassland fringe the city along
the south and north-western
corner. Join us for a day on one
such meadow and discover the
delights of these unique wildlife
treasure troves.

I have arrived early, but many of the
meadow residents have already been
busying themselves for several hours,
including the birds. By this point in early
summer, most of them have secured a
territory and a partner, so the purpose-
driven dawn choruses of spring have
quietened a little, but this can work in
our favour, making it easier to discern
individual voices. With a bit of patience,
even novice birders like me can identify
some common species, and, as I was once
told, you only need to know a few species
to sound impressive.

This morning, one of the easiest to pick out
is the **chiffchaff**, a migrant warbler from the
Mediterranean that constantly repeats its
own name – 'chiff-chaff, chiff-chaff, chiff-
chaff'. This diminutive bird, clad in muted
tones with a lick of pale eyeliner across its
brow, might go unnoticed were it not for this
incessant self-promotion.

Joining the chiffchaff from a nearby treetop
is a **blackcap**; its song begins quietly, with an
almost scratchy tone, before bursting into
a solo of unbridled joy. Sounding a bit like
a blackbird on fast-forward, these happy
warblers can be distinguished by their dark
crowns – black in males and chestnut brown
in females and juveniles.

From an even higher perch, the **song thrush** cuts through the air with bell-like clarity. Its tendency to emphasise a point by repeating phrases two or three times makes it very recognisable. Later in the summer, these speckle-breasted birds may also be overheard smashing snails off large stones to feast on the soft bounty beneath the shells.

**Blue tits, great tits** and **goldfinches** also chatter and call as they flit among the bushes scattered across the meadow. Although not specific to chalk grasslands, all these birds find plenty of food in the abundant insect populations and can also shelter in the scattered scrub patches.

From the dense woodland neighbouring the meadow, I catch sight of a **badger** returning from a nightshift. It cocks its distinctive,

TOP ROW: **SKYLARK; REDWING; BADGER**
BOTTOM ROW: **CHIFFCHAFF; BLACKCAP; LADY'S BEDSTRAW**

striped head for a few seconds, perhaps alerted to my presence, before heading down to the solace of its subterranean home. Although many city dwellers will never have seen a live badger, it remains one of the most recognisable species in Britain. Common residents of chalk grasslands, their presence is often indicated by large piles of chalky rubble unearthed by their powerful paws to create setts. These underground homes, made up of winding tunnels and cavernous hollows, can extend well over 50m (164ft) beneath our feet. Despite living in social groups, known as clans, their arrangement is more like that of housemates, with each individual preferring to forage for food independently. Another giveaway that badgers are nearby is their tidy toileting. If you ever come across a shallow pit with more than one 'deposit', you've likely found a badger latrine. These not only mean that setts remain faeces-free but also serve as a way for clan members to communicate.

As the sun creeps higher and the badgers no doubt drift into snoozy slumber, I venture further into the meadow. Foamy blooms of **lady's bedstraw** perfume the air, and lilac flower heads of field scabious bob on impossibly long stems. These hairy stems are actually responsible for the flower's rather unflattering name – once thought to resemble scabby legs, they were used to treat scabies. The use of plants to treat the

body parts they resembled was common in the 16th and 17th centuries, and renowned London herbalist Nicholas Culpeper included many chalk grassland flowers in his 1653 book *Culpeper's Complete Herbal*.

Unaware of any possible medicinal benefits, the insect throngs simply come to enjoy the nectar buffet, humming and whirring as they jounce from flower to flower and jostle for space on umbellifers. Awake and buzzing in time for breakfast, the appropriately named **marmalade hoverfly** is Britain's most common hoverfly and despite being harmless is often mistaken for a wasp due to its black and gold striped outfit. In fact, the

**COMMON BLUE BUTTERFLY**

different-sized black bands across its body are how it got its name: 'thin cut' and 'thick cut', as with marmalade.

Their gentle drone is joined by the more engine-like churr of bees such as the **red-tailed bumblebee**. One of 24 bumblebee species in Britain, over half of which can be found in London, they dawdle around the meadows, legs often laden with claggy yellow pollen, seeking nectar from plants such as common bird's-foot trefoil. This wonder plant supports over 130 different insect species and is the preferred larval food plant for several butterflies. Its yellow, slipper-like flowers contrasting with red buds have earned it numerous local names including 'eggs and bacon'. Among its golden blooms, a flash of brilliant green – a female **green hairstreak butterfly** is looking for a suitable place to lay her eggs. Her tiny, hairy caterpillars will hatch in a week or so and feast on the tenderest leaves before pupating and remaining hidden in the undergrowth until next summer.

Also competing for the same egg-laying spots is the less visually stunning and aptly named **dingy skipper butterfly**. Its moth-like appearance and darting flight pattern can make it tricky to spot at this time of day, but in late afternoon it is often possible to see several individuals roosting together on dead flower heads. This increasingly rare skipper butterfly has experienced significant population declines in recent decades,

so London's chalk meadows provide an important stronghold for it.

Britain's butterflies are largely sun worshippers, and on a warm, clear day such as this, many of them are basking or putting on their aerial displays. Chalk grassland is one of the best places to enjoy butterfly behaviour, and each species has its own particular style. Gliding effortlessly between its favoured purple flowers, thistles and knapweeds, one of the larger species, a **dark green fritillary**, is first to catch my eye. It is easy to see why this butterfly's scientific name, *Speyeria aglaja*, came from the Greek Aglaea, goddess of beauty, splendour and brightness. Clad in intricate swirls of black and gold, its undersides are studded with pearl-like spots amid patches of the forest green for which it's named.

Far less showy are the delicate **small blue butterflies** clustering on bare patches of damp ground nearby. Jostling for space, each one extracts salts and minerals with its proboscis, a long tongue that coils and uncoils repeatedly like a party blower. No bigger than a thumbnail and more slate-grey than blue, the smallest of Britain's 59 butterfly species thrives on London's chalk grasslands where the sole food plant of their caterpillars can be found – the yellow pompom-like **kidney vetch**. Females can often be seen pirouetting on the fuzzy pincushion flower heads before laying individual eggs deep within.

A relation to the small blue, the **chalkhill blue** is one of several butterflies that are helpfully named after their preferred habitat. The sky-blue males are unmistakable but the less active, muddy brown females can go unnoticed. Like their cousin the large blue, which went extinct in Britain in the 1970s but has successfully been reintroduced in Somerset, the chalkhill blue has a fascinating relationship with ants. During the final stages as a larva, the caterpillar will release a sweet liquid from its honey gland, which ants cannot resist. In exchange for this nectar, the ants will protect the larva, enabling it to safely transition to the next phase of its life cycle, the pupa. The ant-enticing nectar continues to be produced by the pupa, and it is thought the ants then carry the pupa away and bury it underground, where it remains safe until the butterfly is ready to emerge around four weeks later.

The meadow ahead of me is punctuated by many anthills, most likely those of the **yellow meadow ant**. These bumpy hummocks are the result of relentless mining by unseen worker ants. Ants move more soil than any other organism, and each grassy hill contains a busy ant-tropolis of channels and chambers. Warmed by the sun, they are shaped to maintain an optimum temperature, and plant roots offer extra structural support.

Across the field, perched on top of one of the hills, is a **green woodpecker** jabbing its needle-sharp beak repeatedly in and out. Its olive-green plumage is well camouflaged in the grass, but its scarlet-capped head gives it away. Ants in all forms – eggs, grubs and adults – are the woodpecker's favourite foods so the hill provides an irresistible banquet. Most often seen alone, green woodpeckers pair for life but prefer to maintain a long-distance relationship outside the breeding season. They roost quite near to their mate over the winter but will wait until spring before officially reaffirming their close bond. This one shrieks out a laughing 'yaffle' call before flying off in its distinctive, undulating style.

The woodpecker comes to land further up the slope, where pinky-purple lollypop heads of **pyramidal orchids** are poking between clumps of upright brome grass. The term orchid often conjures up images of tropical greenhouses or far-flung places, but Britain is home to 52 different species of wild orchid, many of which can be found on chalk grasslands. Orchid seeds don't store enough food to fully grow into plants, so, like the ants and butterflies, they have formed a symbiotic partnership in order to survive. Fungi growing in the soil feed the orchid seeds, and in return the orchids' roots protect the fungi.

**Bee orchids** are a regular sight in this meadow; they evolved to look like a specific

species of bee they needed for pollination. However, the required species doesn't occur in Britain, so bee orchids here have adapted even further to allow for self-pollination. Each bee orchid spike can have up to ten flowers with pink wing-like sepals and yellow markings on crimson lips. Various other grassland orchid species also display these anthropomorphic (human) or zoomorphic (animal) traits, including the man orchid, fly orchid and greater butterfly-orchid.

Mimicry is common in the natural world, with many insect species also having evolved to look like something or someone else to try to dupe predators. One such example easily found on chalk grasslands is the **wasp spider**. An escapee from the Mediterranean, it is now well established in

TOP ROW: **GREEN WOODPECKER; PYRAMIDAL ORCHID; WASP SPIDER**
BOTTOM ROW: **BUSH CRICKET; COMMON LIZARD; SLOW-WORM**

Britain and the female can be found resting in a web suspended between tall blades of grass. The wasp spider's web has a wide white zigzag stripe down the middle, the function of which is unclear, and spherical egg sacks may be attached nearby. The female's black and yellow stripes confuse predators who mistake it for a real wasp and so steer clear to avoid being stung.

With the sun at its hottest now, the scent of **wild marjoram** floats on the air. This aromatic herb with delicate pink flowers is the same herb as the oregano used in Mediterranean cooking. Flowering alongside it are the buttery blooms of a plant that grows more in London than anywhere else in the country – **greater yellow-rattle**. This scarce and important plant leads a hemiparasitic life (obtaining part of its food by parasitism), feeding on the nutrients of dominant grass roots, thereby weakening them and allowing wildflowers to flourish instead. Later in the summer, the flowers will turn into husks like brown paper bags with rattling seeds inside.

The whirring of winged insects is now joined by the chirping of **meadow grasshoppers** and **bush crickets**, which spring and ping in all directions. Often tricky to tell apart, grasshoppers generally have much shorter antennae than crickets, and the two also use slightly different methods of body percussion to create their characteristic tunes. Crickets 'sing' by rubbing their wings together while grasshoppers rub their legs against their wings.

Soaking up the rays on a nearby fencepost, and possibly eyeing up the grasshoppers as a snack, is a **common lizard**. No longer than a person's index finger, it relies on the sun to warm its tiny body. Lizards have the incredible ability to self-amputate their tails when threatened by predators. The shed tail will continue to move and twitch, distracting the predator, while the important part of the lizard escapes and will eventually grow a new tail.

SKYLARK

Another grassland species capable of tail shedding is the **slow-worm**, which can often be found hiding in warm spots on the meadows throughout the summer months. Despite its name and appearance, it is neither a worm nor a snake, but a legless lizard. Females are recognisable by their rich coppery colour and dark stripes, whereas males are paler and will often have tiny blue spots along their back and sides. This time of year is mating season and males become quite aggressive towards each other in order to secure a mate. Courtship can last for up to ten hours and the female will give birth to live young in late summer.

On the other side of the fence, a small herd of sheep is helping to support the chalk grassland ecosystem. These are **Herdwicks**, the hardy Lake District breed with teddy-bearish faces and mouths that seem to have a permanent half-smile. Their constant nibbling keeps the sward height low, giving grassland flowers the chance to establish; their droppings also help disperse wildflower seeds. Conservation grazing in urban areas like London has increased in recent years with sites using sheep, cattle, horses and even goats to help manage meadows for wildlife and reduce the need to use machinery.

High above the sheep, a hovering **kestrel** hunts for prey. Following a decline in numbers in the 1970s, kestrels began to recover through to the late 1990s, but have since declined again. Although many breeding pairs are resident in London, the loss of brownfield sites, decline in large beetles and small mammals may prevent their longer-term recovery. Detecting their prey with pinpoint accurate eyesight, the kestrels' diet mostly consists of small mammals such as mice and field voles. Despite there being more field voles in Britain than people, with a population of around 75 million, they are seldom seen, as they spend much of their time hidden in vegetation, scurrying along grassy tunnels and feasting on seeds, roots and leaves. Voles are fiercely territorial so while on the move they constantly scent-mark with urine. Unfortunately for the voles, kestrels can see in the ultraviolet light range, so as the urine fluoresces the kestrels are provided with a glowing map leading them straight to their dinner.

A fellow hoverer joining the kestrel is a male **skylark** belting out his symphonic tune. Songs can last for up to an hour with birds reaching heights of up to 300m (1,000ft) before parachuting back to earth. Streaked in shades of brown, skylarks have punky crests that contrast perfectly with their choirboy voices. The subject of many poetic pieces and once synonymous with British meadows, they are now a rare sight and sound, largely due to changes in farming practices reducing suitable habitat. Luckily, conservation efforts on London's meadows are focusing on retaining skylarks in the capital given the impacts of dogs, people and development pressures on nesting sites.

Shadows lengthen slightly as the sun begins to dip. Chequered **marbled white butterflies** and their cousins the **meadow browns** start to find roosting spots on slender stalks, with several individuals often found sharing one stem. Also adorning some of the stems are globules of frothy spume known to many as 'cuckoo spit'. These bubbly blobs house the nymphs of **common froghopper bugs**, who are safely cocooned inside, feeding on plant sap. They use the sap to create their foamy homes by forcing it out of their anuses. Also known as spittlebugs, the adults are high-jump champions, able to leap 70cm (28in) – the equivalent to you or me jumping over a skyscraper.

Scuttling out from the dense undergrowth beneath the froghoppers, a **violet ground beetle** emerges. It is one of many beetle species found on the grasslands, and its purple tinge makes it especially striking. Lively, nocturnal predators, these beetles spend their nights hunting other insects, slugs and worms, although they have to compete for these with small mammals such as common shrews.

The long-snouted, velvety **shrews** live fast and die young, surviving for only a year. Needing to eat every two–three hours during spring and summer, they are extremely active, but during winter their appetites

decrease, as they have the ability to reduce their own size – even their skull and brain. A few lucky people have observed a shrew 'caravan' where a mother shrew leads her young in a line, with each one grasping the tail of the one in front; I live in hope of seeing this shrew conga for myself one day.

At the top of the grassy bank, four **fox** cubs frisk and frolic while their mother looks on, bushy tail wrapped around her haunches. Urban foxes, particularly those in London, divide public opinion, with many believing them to be noisy, bin-rummaging pests. But the meadow foxes are suburban foxes, more cautious than their inner-city counterparts but still comfortable enough with humans to let you observe at a distance. The youngsters leap and snap at passing moths.

Some of the moths could prove quite a mouthful, such as the freshly emerged **privet hawk moth** feeding on hedge honeysuckle. The largest of nine resident species of British hawk moths, this pink-and-black-striped gentle giant spends its short adult life feeding on nectar-rich flowers at night. Its caterpillars, which will emerge later in the summer, are almost as striking as the adults, having diagonal white and purple stripes across their bright green backs. Much maligned, moths are often dismissed as the less attractive relatives of butterflies, but many species are arguably just as beautiful. However, with hundreds of Britain's 2,500 species to be found in London, identifying them is more of a challenge. Moths aren't the only nocturnal insects, and London's chalk meadows are home to several colonies of what has to be one of the capital's most magical insects – **glow-worm**. Hoping to attract a passing male, the tiny females flash their greenish-yellow rear ends throughout June and July. But so far, these unseasonal fairy lights have eluded me, and as I squint into the growing darkness my eyes start to play tricks on me. I wait a bit longer, convinced that as soon as I turn my back the illuminations will begin, but tonight is not the night... maybe next time.

TOP ROW: **SHEEP AT SALTBOX HILL; KESTREL; MARBLED WHITE**
BOTTOM ROW: **MEADOW BROWN; FOX CUB; PRIVET HAWK MOTH**

# THE FALL & RISE OF CHALK GRASSLAND

Britain has lost over 80 per cent of its chalk grassland in the last 75 years. Changes to farming practices, including intensification and increased use of pesticides and fertilisers, have contributed to the loss, as well as pressure from urbanisation and recreation. The chalk grassland habitat relies on a delicate balance of low-nutrient, quick-draining soil that warms up quickly. These 'stressed' conditions allow a hugely diverse range of grassland herbs and wildflowers to prosper, which consequently attracts and supports a varied array of wildlife. With up to 40 different species to be found in just one square meter (up to 37 species in a square yard) of chalk grassland, conserving these valuable habitats is essential.

Small areas of habitat, far from others, can lead to species populations becoming isolated and eventually dying out. By conserving and restoring existing meadows and working together with local communities to create a living landscape of interconnectivity between these meadows, species can succeed and their distributions can spread.

The future is looking brighter, with large-scale landscape projects taking place that focus on protecting and promoting chalk grassland. There are also valuable smaller-scale interventions, such as changing local mowing regimes to allow areas of insect-rich grassland to remain for most of the year, and encouraging people to devote areas of their gardens and balconies to wildflowers.

# A FEW OF THE BEST CHALK GRASSLANDS IN LONDON

'It is interesting to contemplate a tangled bank, clothed with many plants of many kinds, with birds singing on the bushes, with various insects flitting about, and with worms crawling through the damp earth, and to reflect that these elaborately constructed forms, so different from each other, and dependent upon each other in so complex a manner, have all been produced by laws acting around us.' Charles Darwin

Charles Darwin's wise words are from his most famous work, *On the Origin of Species*, published in 1859, and are thought to refer to the chalk grassland slopes surrounding his home in Downe, now in the London Borough of Bromley. This is one of five London boroughs in which chalk grassland meadows can be found, along with Croydon, Sutton, Lewisham and Hillingdon. The combined area totals around 390 hectares (964 acres) and makes up just over 3 per cent of the total area of chalk grassland found in southeast England. The following are some of the best sites to experience the grassland for yourself.

# Hutchinson's Bank
## New Addington, Croydon

Just a few minutes from New Addington,
this Local Nature Reserve is a butterfly-
spotter's paradise. The rolling landscape
on this 14-hectare (35-acre) corner of the
North Downs is home to up to 40 different
butterfly species throughout the year.
The site also benefits from grazing sheep,
and surrounding ancient woodland areas
provide an additional habitat to explore.

## Downe Bank
### Bromley

Also part of the North Downs, this 5-hectare (12-acre) site is where Charles Darwin carried out some of his fundamental scientific studies. Darwin's home, Down House, is nearby. Downe Bank – which was known to him as 'Orchis Bank' thanks to the large variety of wild orchids, including common fragrant-orchid – is a uniquely special nature reserve by virtue of its status as part of Darwin's 'landscape laboratory'.

## Riddlesdown Common
### Kenley, Croydon

The single largest area – 43 hectares (106 acres) – of chalk grassland in Greater London can be found here, a Site of Special Scientific Interest. The site is steeped in history, with evidence of activity dating back to the Stone Age and a Roman road running through it. Criss-crossed with walking trails that allow for excellent wildlife spotting, the area is also roamed by grazing sheep and cattle.

# Roundshaw Downs
## Sutton

This large area – 38 hectares (94 acres) – of chalk grassland has had a varied and interesting past. Once farmland, it was then transformed into Croydon Airport in the 1920s, London's only international airport at the time. The Downs were notified as a Local Nature Reserve in 1994 and now boasts a wide variety of wildlife including meadow pipits and skylarks.

# Dollypers Hill
## Old Coulsdon, Croydon

This 12-hectare (30-acre) nature oasis is nestled between suburban housing estates, but once you are enveloped in one of its grassland glades, you'll feel very far from urban civilisation. Historically the area was farmed as common land, punctuated with chalk pits, and much of it has returned to secondary woodland, but restoration works have meant that species-rich meadows now cover a significant proportion of the site.

# Marbled white: a butterfly on the up

*The State of the UK's Butterflies 2015* report showed that there had been a staggering 76 per cent loss in abundance or occurrence of the country's butterfly species over the previous four decades. However, some species are bucking this disheartening trend. The marbled white *Melanargia galathea* showed a 50 per cent increase in the same time period and hugely expanded its range, too. Once confined to central and southern areas of Britain, this unmistakable species can now be found as far north as Yorkshire. Climate change is thought to be the main driver behind the increase, and with urban city environments providing even warmer temperatures, London has proved to be a hot spot of significant success for this species. Sightings in the capital used to be restricted to boroughs on the outer fringes, but in Inner London boroughs, including Tower Hamlets, Southwark and Westminster, sightings have been increasing year on year.

Butterflies are by far the most studied and recorded insects in Britain, providing valuable insights into species trends and the wider impacts on biodiversity associated with these trends. The marbled white is now included in the annual citizen science project the Big Butterfly Count, which encourages members of the public to spend time recording butterflies in gardens and local green spaces; this not only builds a picture of different species across London and nationally but also allows people to experience the positive wellbeing benefits of butterfly spotting.

The name marbled white is something of a misnomer as the butterfly is actually a member of the subfamily commonly known as the 'browns', subfamily Satyrinae. The Satyrids get their name from a pair of tail points their caterpillars have which are thought to resemble the ears of a woodland deity from Greek mythology known as a satyr. The two-tone chequerboard wings of the marbled white gave rise to early names, including 'Our Half Mourner' given by London naturalist James Petiver in 1695. The genus, Melanargia, comes from melas (black) and arges (brightness). Their striking patterning is thought to be aposematic – it warns predators, such as birds, of their distastefulness. Although not fully understood, research suggests that a fungus present in some of the grasses the caterpillars feed on leads to a build-up of a chemical that tastes disgusting to birds.

It's a wonder that any make it to the caterpillar stage, as female marbled whites have a rather slapdash approach to egg laying; instead of individually positioning eggs, they just release them one at a time and let them drop to the ground. Once hatched a few weeks later, the caterpillars eat their eggshells before promptly entering a hibernation stage, tucked away in deep vegetation until the following spring. Sometime in May the caterpillars will pupate, having feasted on a range of grasses including red fescue, Yorkshire fog and tor-grass.

Adults will start emerging from around mid-June and remain on the wing until early August. Despite this fleetingly short flight period, you stand a good chance of seeing one on warm, sunny days in London, most likely feeding on their favourite purple blooms such as knapweed, scabious, thistles and buddleia. Their preference for calcareous (chalky) soils means large colonies can be found on London's chalk grassland meadows, particularly in Bromley, Croydon and Sutton, where over 150 individuals were counted in under an hour on one site in 2020. However, because of the varied diet of its caterpillars, smaller colonies can exist on any patches of unimproved grassland where grasses grow

tall, including areas left unmown on road verges, along railway lines, in parks and in private gardens.

London's extensive transport network and plethora of urban parks, as well as a growing awareness of the need to leave areas of grass and wildflowers uncut, are starting to provide a network of habitats to link marbled white colonies. Their adaptability in taking advantage of the urban environment, alongside rising temperatures, continues to fuel this species' growing success across London and should hope to ensure a bright future for one of Britain's most attractive butterflies.

# Greater knapweed: a bold meadow gem

The punky, purple mop-tops of greater knapweed *Centaurea scabiosa* provide some of the brightest splashes of colour on London's chalk grasslands from June all the way through to September. A member of the daisy (Asteraceae) family, it can grow up to 1.2m (4ft) tall, often towering over other grassland wildflowers. Each of the large blooms is, in fact, a composite flower head made up of a crown of infertile, ragged bracts surrounding the inner, fertile florets. They provide a fantastic source of nectar and pollen, and the large, bright flowers make them highly attractive to a wide range of insects – marbled white, meadow brown and green-veined white butterflies can often be seen clustered on one flower head on warm summer days.

Knapweeds are often confused with thistles, but their dark green, almost leathery, leaves and stems lack the spines and bristles found on thistles. They are, however, covered in downy hairs, which led to both the stems and leaves once being used by herbalists in the capital to treat the skin infection scabies. From this practice the plant got part of its botanical name: scabiosa.

Many common local names are known, including hardhead, ironhead, bullweed and bottleweed, which are thought to relate

to the sturdy nature of the plant and the base of its flower head (involucre) which is globular and bottle-shaped. The involucres are made up from a decorative rosette of overlapping, fringed bracts that strongly resemble artichokes (also members of the Asteraceae family). The bracts spread apart during seeding to produce downy, silver star shapes very similar to a classic daisy shape. As an added benefit to wildlife, the seeds of greater knapweed are enjoyed by birds, including goldfinches and chaffinches.

Thought to have originated on the steppes (flat grasslands) in Russia, greater knapweed thrives in low-fertility soil, and London's chalk meadows are among the best places to see them and all their associated wildlife. However, they also grow very well along road verges and railway lines so commuters should keep an eye out for them. The fringes of roads and railways criss-crossing the city can help to create a vital network to support the recovery of nature; if these areas are managed appropriately, wildflowers can flourish. To reinforce this point further, a rare white form of greater knapweed called albiflora was actually discovered on a road verge in 1980.

Both greater knapweed and its close relative common, or black knapweed *Centaurea*

*nigra* are on the Royal Horticultural Society's 'Plants for Pollinators' list, which hopes to inspire people to grow a range of year-round flowering plants that support bees, hoverflies, butterflies and other pollinators. The flamboyance of knapweeds makes them an excellent addition to gardens and allotments in London – they do very well in sunny borders and often grow a lot larger than they do in the wild. With as many Londoners as possible acting as 'insect champions', planting species such as knapweed and encouraging local councils to manage road verges for wildlife, the loss of species-rich grasslands and the 50 per cent decline in insects seen in just the last 50 years can start to be reversed.

## NOTES

# Chapter 9

BY EDWIN MALINS

# TOP 10 HIDDEN GEMS

As the winter turns to spring, this yellow carpet gives way to bluebells, banks of purple foxgloves and aromatic wild garlic.

# Lesnes Abbey Wood

*(Bexley Council)* ♦ *Food and drink are available from the Chestnuts Kiosk* ♦ *The nearest railway station is Abbey Wood, 500 metres away in the suburb named after this site.*

**GREAT FOR**

*Sweet chestnut*
*Birch*
*Oak*
*Wild daffodils*
*Bluebells*
*Foxgloves*
*Wild garlic*
*Butterflies*
*Buzzards*
*Fossils*
*Lichens*

A riot of woodland wildflower colour in spring, this wonderful 88-hectare (217-acre) woodland is the best place in London to enjoy wild daffodils in bloom. The mixture of ancient woodland, with patches of restored heathland, meadow, ponds, parkland and formal garden, not to mention the ruins of an ancient abbey, makes this a perfect space to explore.

The woodland is a mixture of sweet chestnut, birch and oak, and it first bursts into life in February and March as the wild daffodils begin flowering. As winter turns to spring, this yellow carpet gives way to bluebells, banks of purple foxgloves and aromatic wild garlic with its delicate white flowers. Small heath butterflies dance across the heathland areas, while buzzards drift over the meadows or perch on the woodland edges hoping to spot a shrew or vole.

Lesnes Abbey Wood is a treasure trove of fossils, and children can explore the fossil pit where they may discover shells from the Eocene (54.5 million years ago). The ruins of the Abbey itself date back to 1178, built by Richard de Luci, possibly as penance for his role in the murder of the Archbishop of Canterbury Thomas Becket. Look out for weird and wonderful lichens growing on the ruins. Lichens are a mutually beneficial partnership between fungi and algae – the fungus provides the structure while the alga obtains energy from the sun. Many lichens are sensitive to air pollution and their presence therefore can be an indicator of good air quality.

The site is managed by Bexley Council with a local 'friends of' group, and has benefitted in recent years from a National Lottery Heritage Fund grant.

# Gunnersbury Triangle

*(London Wildlife Trust/Hounslow Council)* ◆ *Chiswick Park station is opposite. Refreshments can be found at cafés on Chiswick High Road, less than 500m (a third of a mile) distant.*

**GREAT FOR**

*Willow*

*Birch*

*Oak*

*Woodpecker*

*Sparrowhawk*

*Frog*

*Toad*

*Newt*

*Slowworm*

Tucked away in the nook between two intersecting railway lines in Chiswick (a disused spur of railway line forming the third side of the triangle), this 3-hectare (7½-acre) Local Nature Reserve is testament to how wildlife can spring back to life in the urban landscape. Having taken over abandoned allotments between the railway tracks, self-sown willows, birch and oak form the backdrop of this enchanting nature reserve, with grassland glades and ponds adding to its diversity. The Triangle's survival is testimony to a campaign by local people in the early 1980s, and a landmark planning decision of 1983 to protect its ecological value for the community.

With its currently unassuming entrance (a new visitor centre is planned) almost opposite Chiswick Park Underground station, Gunnersbury Triangle is easy to get to. Its single entrance path unfurls into a wider network criss-crossing the site, which make for an immersive atmosphere, despite the regularly passing trains.

Springtime in the dense woodland brings with it a flurry of birdsong, woodpecker drumming and occasional hunting forays from sparrowhawk. The ponds are havens for frogs, toads and smooth newt, while out in the acid grassland meadow you might be lucky enough to catch a glimpse of a slow-worm (actually a harmless, legless lizard). This species has recently colonised the reserve of its own accord, journeying along the railway lines to take advantage of a habitat seemingly created with its sun-loving lifestyle in mind.

The Triangle has been managed by London Wildlife Trust on behalf of Hounslow Council since 1985, with the support of an active group of local volunteers.

Birch and oak
form the backdrop
of this enchanting
nature reserve,
with grassland
glades and ponds
adding to its
diversity.

London is fortunate to have many surviving fragments of ancient woodland, and Biggin Wood is a peaceful and unassuming example.

# Biggin Wood

*(Croydon Council)* ◆ *Norbury railway station is about 2km (just over 1 mile) away.*

**GREAT FOR**

*Phoenix tree*
*Stag beetle*

Woodlands in urban areas can suffer from intense visitor pressure, but the 5.2-hectare (13-acre) Biggin Wood is typically quieter than the nearby Streatham Common woodland, and Dulwich & Sydenham Hill Woods.

What Biggin Wood has in common with its woodland neighbours, however, is that they once formed part of a larger whole – the Great North Wood. This patchwork of coppiced woodlands and wooded commons covered the high ground from Deptford to Selhurst for centuries until it largely made way for London's expansion. The North Wood (the epithet 'Great' being a Victorian addition) was so called as it lay to the north of the market town of Croydon.

Parts of Biggin Wood formed the grounds of a big house (quirks of ownership often explain the survival of urban woodlands) and although the house was destroyed in a fire long ago, some traces of Victorian horticulture can still be found in the wood, such as a large holly with pretty, variegated leaves. Close to this holly, you can find an enormous fallen field maple, a phoenix tree that continues to live where it has toppled, and bluebells grow from the mound its descent created.

One of London's most charismatic insects, the stag beetle, lives in Biggin Wood. You will never see its larvae, as they live for up to seven years in rotting tree stumps, feeding on the wood. But if you visit Biggin Wood on a balmy evening in late June or early July, you may be treated to the magnificence of the adult stage of the beetles in their flight season. Their brief moment in the sun as adults is the culmination of years of preparation. They are harmless to us and seem not to be bothered by our presence.

# Gutteridge Wood & Ten Acre Wood

*(London Wildlife Trust/Hillingdon Council)*
*• Hillingdon Underground is about 12 minutes' walk away.*

**GREAT FOR**

*Willow*
*Birch*
*Oak*
*Woodpecker*
*Sparrowhawk*
*Frog*
*Toad*
*Newt*
*Slowworm*

The River Crane is one of London's more intact river valleys. In its northern reaches, where it branches into the Yeading Brooks, the floodplain of the river still feels remarkably rural. Gutteridge Wood and Ten Acre Wood are good places to experience this, as the Brook wends its way through a vibrant landscape of woodland and meadow.

Gutteridge Wood, which is a 25-hectare (62-acre) site, can be accessed from the adjacent Lyndhurst Crescent and Elephant Park, where the Hillingdon Trail, a long-distance footpath, enters the woodland from the west.

At its core, the wood is ancient (meaning that it has been wooded continuously since 1600), something that is indicated by its impressive carpet of spring flowers. Hidden within the woodland are two meadows, one large and one small. At the height of summer, in the midst of wildflowers and insects, and flanked on all sides by woodland, you would not know you are still in suburbia and just a short distance from the A40 as it roars out of London to the west.

The Hillingdon Trail connects Gutteridge Wood to Ten Acre Wood – which, despite its name is 11 hectares (27 acres) – passing by two further meadows and across some fields with beautiful mature oak trees in the overgrown hedgerows. Along with Gutteridge Wood, this is a Local Nature Reserve. In late spring listen out for a cuckoo in the hedgerow, or the high-pitched conversation of long-tailed tits in the tree canopy.

Crossing the Yeading Brook to enter Ten Acre Wood, you can make this into a circular walk by starting with the longer route through the woodland and then heading back along the shorter route adjacent to the river. Ten Acre Wood is a plantation of oaks and is not classed as ancient. If you have come in springtime you will be able to

In late spring listen out for a cuckoo in the hedgerow, or the high-pitched conversation of long-tailed tits in the tree canopy.

its less colourful understorey with Gutteridge Wood's display of bluebells. At the southern end of the site is a large meadow often grazed by cattle in the late summer, and you can continue your walk to the south if you wish to follow the Hillingdon Trail onwards to Yeading Brook Meadows, a fantastic site for wildflowers and skylark.

The open meadow slopes of Wood Farm make it a good place to spot butterflies in the summer months.

# Wood Farm
# & Stanmore Country Park

*(Harrow Council) ◆ Both sites are walkable from Stanmore*
*Underground station.*

A truly commanding view across north London can be found at the Wood Farm viewpoint, and you might also spot kestrel, buzzard, red kite and sparrowhawk hunting across the meadows. Wood Farm was indeed a farm until very recently, only being opened to the public in 2015. Owned by Harrow Council, it is now looked after by volunteers from the Harrow Nature Conservation Forum.

The open meadow slopes of Wood Farm make it a good place to spot butterflies in the summer months, including clouded yellow, which migrates here from southern Europe and northern Africa each year, a remarkable feat for a small insect. Although some clouded yellows are seen every year in Britain, numbers vary greatly. When the conditions are right, they can arrive on our shores in huge numbers, providing a dazzling display of colour.

On lower ground to the south, Stanmore Country Park combines acid grasslands peppered with numerous anthills and damp woodlands adorned with ferns. Green woodpeckers forage for ants and other insects across the meadows. In April, the blackthorns are flush with white blossom, marking the start of spring. Blackthorn is a very spiky bush, but its flowers are delicate and eventually turn into the distinctive blue fruit known as sloes, which look like tiny plums. These are exceedingly bitter but are used to flavour specialist sloe gins.

If you have time for a longer walk, you could keep going further north to find Bentley Priory and Stanmore Common, both wonderful wildlife sites also managed by local volunteers.

# Beckton Creekside nature reserve

*(Thames Water)* ◆ *Barking station is the nearest at 5km (3 miles) away.*

**GREAT FOR**

*Reed warbler*
*Sedge warbler*
*Little egret*
*Grey wagtail*
*Dragonflies*
*Buzzard*
*Kestrel*
*Sparrowhawk*
*Barn owl*

Wildlife thrives at this nature reserve, which is tucked away alongside Beckton Sewage Treatment Works, one of the largest facilities of its kind in the country. Sitting close to the River Roding, where it completes its journey through east London down to meet the Thames, this site is a reminder of the value of industrial landscapes for wildlife in the city.

In the spring and summer months, reed warblers and sedge warblers breed in the reedbeds, having spent the previous winter in Africa. Listen out for the mellow, churring song of the reed warbler or the more frantic, electric sounds of the sedge warbler. These birds feed on insects, and the British spring/summer provides perfect conditions for them to raise their young in the profusion of insects that emerge as our weather gets warmer. In the winter, they are better served by seeking out warmer weather in more tropical climates.

Down at the water's edge, you may spot little egret, a brilliant white member of the heron family, foraging in the shallows. Grey wagtail (a confusing name as it has flashes of yellow) may also be seen bobbing around in the shallows. Keep an eye out for dragonflies hunting around the nature reserve, as well as a suite of common butterfly species that are on the wing in the summer months.

Look out for buzzard, kestrel and sparrowhawk silhouetted against the skies or perching on infrastructure above, as they hunt across the reserve, sewage works and surrounding landscape. There is also a healthy population of barn owls close by (a rarity in London), and although you are unlikely to see them, it is comforting to know that they thrive in this corner of east London.

BARN OWL

Listen out for the mellow, churring song of the reed warbler or the more frantic, electric sounds of the sedge warbler.

Bring a pair of binoculars along and try to spot some of the Reservoir's charismatic water birds... Tufted ducks are an easy species to identify, with their bright eyes and the extravagant head-tuft on the male birds.

# Welsh Harp (Brent) Reservoir

*(Canal & River Trust, and Barnet & Brent councils)* ◆ *Hendon railway station is about 500m (a third of a mile) from the northern end, and Wembley Park Underground station is about 1.5km (1 mile) from the south-western end of the reservoir.*

GREAT FOR

*Great crested grebe*
*Tufted duck*
*Grey heron*
*Butterflies*
*Dragonflies*
*Damselflies*
*Lime trees*

The Welsh Harp is named after the pub that once stood nearby, is surprisingly little-known by Londoners despite its formidable size of 69 hectares (170 acres). It is designated as a Site of Special Scientific Interest and part of a larger Local Nature Reserve. The Brent Reservoir was created in 1834–5 by flooding farmland adjacent to the River Brent in order to create a water supply for the Grand Union and Regent's Canals. It suffers from large amounts of rubbish being brought downstream in the River Brent and Silk Stream, which flow into it, but this doesn't detract from its wonderful resident and visiting birdlife, nor the sheer scale of this waterbody and the vista it provides across to Wembley Stadium. This is particularly evocative as the sun sets over northwest London.

Bring a pair of binoculars along if you can, and try to spot some of the Reservoir's charismatic water birds. Early in the breeding season you might spot the courtship rituals of the great-crested grebe, a species that has recovered from past declines that resulted from its popularity as a source of feathers for hats. Tufted ducks are an easy species to identify, with their bright eyes and the extravagant head-tuft on the male birds. You might also spot a grey heron hunting in the shallows, or standing completely motionless, almost statuesque.

The land surrounding the Reservoir, including the Welsh Harp Open Space, has a mixture of meadows and woodland to enjoy. In midsummer you can find butterflies such as ringlet and marbled white dancing across the meadows, or iridescent dragonflies and damselflies, sometimes locked in a mating embrace. Tucked away in the woodlands are common lime trees with vigorous and dense shoots coming out of the base. Although not uncommon in this tree species, these are extreme examples, and create an ethereal, almost gothic, atmosphere on a misty day.

# Hutchinson's Bank

*(London Wildlife Trust/Croydon Council)* • *Hutchinson's Bank is 500 metres (a third of a mile) from New Addington Tramlink station.*

**GREAT FOR**

*Butterflies*
*Kidney vetch flower*
*Common lizard*
*Kestrel*
*Buzzard*
*Solitary bees*
*Greater yellow-rattle*
*Orchids*

Well-known among butterfly enthusiasts, these chalk slopes on the edge of Greater London remain a hidden gem as yet undiscovered by many Londoners. Late spring and summer are the best times of year to visit in order to marvel at the density and diversity of the butterfly populations, while early spring is ideal to enjoy the blossom in the scrub surrounding the grasslands.

Entering the 22-hectare (54-acre) Local Nature Reserve from this end initially brings you into the patchwork of grazed grassland paddocks, scrub borders and bisecting footpath trails. The butterfly highlight of this section is known as The Cutting, earthworks from an incomplete crescent of 1930s housing, initially paused by World War II and then prevented from progress by post-war Green Belt legislation. This suntrap, sheltered from the wind, creates a microclimate that plays host to a multitude of butterflies. On a summer's day you will often find enthusiastic amateur butterfly experts here, who may be keen to share their knowledge and let you know what they have seen so far that day.

Further to the south, the hillside of Slimmings' Down slopes away towards the ancient woodland of Threecorner Grove. At the bottom of the hill you will find a sea of kidney vetch flowers occupying an area carefully created with machinery. Britain's smallest butterfly, the small blue, can be found in large numbers across this yellow-flecked carpet of kidney vetch flowers, where it lays its eggs for the next generation of caterpillars to feed. On bare rock scattered across this area you may also spot common lizards basking, and don't forget to check the skies above you from time to time for a hovering kestrel or buzzard drifting across the valley.

Late spring and summer are the best times of year to visit in order to marvel at the density and diversity of the butterfly populations.

SMALL BLUE
BUTTERFLY

We are used to having our view obscured by buildings, trees and hills, but here the flat and open vista allows us to appreciate the sky in its enormity.

GRASS SNAKE

# Walthamstow Marshes

*(Lee Valley Regional Park Authority)* • *From Clapton railway station, it's about 1.5km (1 mile) to Walthamstow Marshes.*

**GREAT FOR**

*Grass snake*
*Water vole*
*Kestrel*
*Meadow pipit*
*Sedge & reed warblers*
*Snipe*
*Dragonflies*
*Creeping marshwort*

These remnants of London's river floodplain grasslands make for a fascinating walk, and demonstrate how river valleys help to keep wildlife interconnected in the urban landscape. Parts of the Marshes are now grazed again to help conserve the open habitats (often by Belted Galloway cattle), harking back to centuries gone by when this would have been common practice. From a distance, you can also imagine these magnificent animals' prehistoric wild ancestors (aurochs) coming down to the river in their herds to drink and feed.

On a visit to the 36.7-hectare (91-acre) Marshes, a Site of Special Scientific Interest (and is the nearby Walthamstow Wetlands), one of the features that is most striking to an urban dweller is its 'big sky' landscape. We are used to having our horizon obscured by buildings, trees and hills, but here the flat and open vista allows us to appreciate the sky, whether grey or blue, in its enormity.

To the north of the grazed fields, you can find a labyrinth of paths running between scrub, glades and ponds. The fertility of the soil here has allowed a profusion of plants that are most certainly not rare, but are the hardy urban colonisers of land that people leave untouched. Nature has a phenomenal ability to recover and take hold in cities if we give it a chance, and this little patch of land is a classic of the genre.

Some of the animals found on the Marshes that are relatively uncommon across the capital include the (non-venomous) grass snake and the water vole. Catching a glimpse of a water vole is a real privilege, as they are very elusive animals. However, they leave us little clues to their presence, such as their droppings which resemble (in shape) Tic Tac mints, or their habit of chewing blades of grasses at a 45-degree angle.

# Forest Hill to New Cross Gate railway corridor

*(Network Rail/Lewisham Council/London Wildlife Trust)* ◆ *Stations at Brockley, Honor Oak Park and Forest Hill are all within 1km (two thirds of a mile) of various accessible parts.*

Railway lines can be one of the city's corridors for wildlife, linear havens sweeping across the urban landscape. One of the best examples in London is the railway line between New Cross Gate and Forest Hill, a designated Site of Metropolitan Importance for Nature Conservation. Created in 1838–9 along much of the route of the short-lived Croydon Canal, this largely wooded stretch of lineside (land adjacent to a railway track) now supports four separate nature reserves, which are all worth a visit. Each one is accessible only on designated open days, and so advance planning is required.

The most northerly site is New Cross Gate Cutting, managed by London Wildlife Trust since 1987, between New Cross Gate and Brockley stations. From the entrance on Vesta Road, a circular walk will take you through shady woodland alive with birdsong, as well as sunny glades buzzing with insect life. Growing from the paths you can find the broad-leaved helleborine, an orchid which is not particularly common in London, as well as stinking iris, which smells like a packet of beef-flavoured crisps when crushed in the hand.

Further south, between Brockley and Honor Oak Park, is Buckthorne Cutting nature reserve, established in 2018 and managed by the Fourth Reserve Foundation. At the northern end of this young woodland of cherry, sycamore, oak and ash is a surprise – a large reedbed. Remnants of reedbed can be seen along this railway corridor (possibly linked to the old canal), but this is the most impressive.

On either side of the line between Forest Hill and Honor Oak Park are Devonshire Road and Garthorne Road nature reserves, managed by local 'friends of' groups on behalf of Lewisham Council. These two sites, that opened in the mid-1980s, are wooded, but also have large wild meadow areas, best enjoyed in the summer months.

Once the route of the short-lived
Croydon Canal, this largely
wooded stretch of lineside has
four different nature reserves,
which are all worth a visit.

# THE FUTURE OF NATURE CONSERVATION: A YOUNG LONDONER'S VIEW BY KABIR KAUL

London has always been my home. As a Londoner with a passion for wildlife, I have discovered and become fascinated with the ecosystems and species found within our great urban jungle. As the population of our capital grows and an ecological crisis looms, the responsibility to maintain this patchwork of green and blue spaces is essential, and it lies with each of us as individuals.

If we are to make our city greener and wilder, Londoners of all ages must first understand the importance of the urban environment on their doorstep. More initiatives run by local councils could encourage residents to make a difference for nature in their local areas, even with something as simple as hanging bird feeders or planting wildflowers. These initiatives could also promote the vital work of 'friends' groups, informing residents about the benefits of volunteering at local green space. Although this is already being carried out in certain areas of the capital, more projects to connect residents with nature must take place across London, to enable more Londoners to notice and appreciate the natural world around them, and unite us with a common understanding of our urban biodiversity.

Once this common understanding has been achieved, we can all engage together in large-scale projects to protect, rewild and maintain our capital's habitats and wildlife. I would like to imagine a network of green corridors, linking streets, neighbourhoods, green spaces and nature reserves stretching across the capital in the future. If London's ecosystems, present and future, are to be places where people and wildlife can thrive together, the continued collaboration of conservation organisations, local authorities and local communities alike will be key. This will ensure that everyone's individual skills and ideas can be used to create a greener, wilder capital, and that more of our built environment can be used to benefit nature.

In addition to the maintenance of our existing ecosystems, greater awareness and stronger laws are needed to preserve our local green spaces, including those that are already threatened. The rapid expansion of urban sprawl over the past few centuries has seen habitats being built upon, leading to the decline of countless mammals, birds and plants. If individual Londoners have developed not just an understanding of the nature on their doorstep but also a passion for it, they will be motivated to make a difference to protect their local green spaces for the future. Moreover, I've known of several green spaces in the past that have been threatened by development despite threatened species living and breeding there – stronger laws will be crucial in protecting the capital's rarest animals and plants, as well as the green spaces they flourish in.

For all of this to be successful, the involvement of London's young people will be essential. In a few decades' time, my generation will carry the immense responsibility of looking after our capital's unique environment, including all its species. Learning about the natural world must be set into our curriculum, starting in primary school. This could include learning how to identify common animals and plants, along with visiting local ecosystems, which would instil in them a love of nature from an early age. To make sure this continues into secondary school, I would hope to see more initiatives encouraging students to volunteer in local green spaces and take part in citizen science surveys. With proposals being considered for a General Certificate of Secondary Education exam in Natural History, I feel more optimistic that young Londoners may have a chance to

immerse themselves in the natural world, equipped with the knowledge they need to maintain our unique environment for tomorrow's Londoners. As we face an ecological crisis, it will be the actions of London's young people that will determine the future of the capital's biodiversity and habitats.

I am hopeful for the future of conservation in London. Through awareness, education and collaboration, all Londoners will have the potential to make a difference to maintain our beautiful urban jungle. If we give today's young people the skills and knowledge to continue this, we can coexist with our capital's biodiversity for generations to come.

# HOW-TO GUIDES

## ...help birds avoid windows

Birds can sometimes struggle to navigate our urban world. Help them out by creating a window feature.

**1.** Sketch a large bird shape on some card, shade it in black, and cut it out.

**2.** Make a hole in the top of the bird shape and tie it to some thread.

**3.** Hang the bird shape outside your window. Breaking up reflections helps birds avoid bumping into the window.

# ...make a pond

As a budding wildlife gardener myself, I'll be making my own mini-pond over the summer, so here are my tips for this project if you want to make a pond yourself. It can seem like a daunting challenge to provide an effective haven if you have a small space. But research has shown that even tiny ponds can contribute towards biodiversity on a regional scale, because they act as stepping stones and allow species to move through the landscape. In the urban setting, where there can be many barriers to wildlife, this is crucial.

## 1. SELECT A CONTAINER

You can basically use anything! This is a great opportunity for upcycling, so look for containers that are roughly 30cm (12in) deep and watertight (or make it watertight using a small piece of pond liner). Choose a spot for your container that gets a good amount of light ,and think about how creatures will be able to get in and out of it. You could dig your container into the ground and provide access levels in and out, or you could build a ramp.

## 2. FILL IT UP

Prepare the vessel using some gravel on the bottom, and then use rocks or logs to create a range of depths. Finally, allow your pond to fill with rainwater. (Avoid tap water as it contains chemicals that may not be conducive to pond life.)

## 3. CHOOSE SOME PLANTS

For a mini-pond, it makes sense to stick to one submerged plant and then you can gradually build up the surrounding area with other freshwater plants. Marsh-marigold/Kingcup is a great choice for a submerged plant, as it provides cover for amphibians and an early nectar source for insects. A personal favourite of mine is the yellow iris, with its sword-shaped leaves and flowers shaped like fleurs-de-lis. Beware, though – it has invasive tendencies and can take over a small pond, so planting it in a separate basket can make it easier to control. Great things to plant around your pond margin are watermint, brooklime and purple loosestrife.
*By former Keeping it Wild trainee, Dexter*

# ...garden when you don't have a garden

◆ Even without a garden you can still do your bit for nature. Salads and herbs grow well from seed in windowsill pots, and their flowers are great for insects. Try mint, sage, thyme and rosemary for starters.

◆ If you have a balcony, you can try growing vegetables such as cherry tomatoes and chard in pots, or fruits like strawberries.

◆ If growing food isn't your thing, think about Mediterranean plants such as lavender or coastal plants like sedums. They grow well in pots and are adored by bees. Remember that plants in pots need regular watering and may need shielding from the wind. Climbers like honeysuckle can be planted in pots to grow up a sunny balcony wall. They are great for attracting bees in the summer, plus warblers and thrushes love to snack on honeysuckle berries.

*By Jo Wright, Centre for Wildlife Gardening*

# ...build a bug hotel

## YOU WILL NEED
Old wooden pallets
Empty bottles
Cardboard
Bamboo canes/plastic straws
Straw, leaves or loose bark
Pebbles, stones or
    bits of broken terracotta pots
Bricks

## FINDING THE IDEAL SPOT FOR YOUR BUG HOTEL

To cater for as many different types of invertebrates as possible, try to find a spot in partial sun, with a little shade. Some invertebrates prefer the sun, while others like cool, damp conditions. You will need a level, even surface on which to build your bug hotel – it may end up quite heavy, so a solid base is important.

**1.** Start by placing the wooden pallet in your chosen spot. Line the top of the wooden pallet with bricks, laying them around the corners and across the middle.

**2.** Place the next pallet on top of this and repeat this process for all of your pallets.

**3.** Next, mark a line around the top two-third of each of your bottles and cut this section off. Fill up half of them with rolled-up cardboard and the other half with plastic straws or bamboo canes. Place these inside the bug hotel.

**4.** Use leaves, bricks, pebbles, stones, loose bark, straw and bits of broken terracotta pots to fill the remaining space. Include any extra material that you would like to recycle such as carpeting, toilet rolls or piping.

**5.** Add a creative flourish – name your hotel and create a sign, ready to welcome your first guests!

# CONTRIBUTORS

**Mathew Frith**
- ◆ **Introduction**
- ◆ **Wild nightlife & urban wildlife**
- ◆ **The future of nature conservation**

An urban ecologist with an interest in the relationship between nature and society in towns and cities, Mathew is currently Director of Research and Policy at London Wildlife Trust, with over 30 years' experience, managing land, advocating for the protection and creation of natural greenspaces, and engaging thousands of people on the wonders of London's wildlife. His favourite spaces in London include Croham Hurst and Isleworth Ait, and he has fondness for crows, beetles, street weeds and wastelands.

**Amy Pryor**
- ◆ **The River Thames**

Amy Pryor is a marine and estuarine scientist with over 20 years of experience in marine and coastal management. She is the Technical Director at Thames Estuary Partnership, and Chairs the national Coastal Partnerships Network. Amy is a lifelong ocean lover, striving to enhance the health of the ocean including the Thames, London's 'local ocean'.

**Peter Massini**
- ◆ **Created Spaces**

Peter started his career as an ecologist by working for London Wildlife Trust from 1987–97. He subsequently worked for the London Ecology Unit, Natural England and the Greater London Authority. Now freelance, one of his clients is the London Wildlife Trust consultancy.

**Sourabh Padke**
- ◆ **Community gardens**

Sourabh is a recent Londoner (three years old and counting). He is an architect/ schoolteacher from India and has previously worked on several community conservation/ environmental education efforts. He has been involved in community gardening projects in London alongside his studies.

**Tim Webb**
- ◆ **The glory of parks**

Tim is a Trustee of both the National Park City Foundation and London Parks and Gardens Trust. As Secretary to the UK Urban Ecology Forum, he was one of the few UK representatives at the UN's World Urban Forum in Abu Dhabi in February 2020.

**Edwin Malins**
◆ **Nature reserves & city farms**
◆ **Top 10 hidden gems**
Edwin is nature reserves manager at London Wildlife Trust.

**Ian Holt – London's heathlands**
Ian is the estate Estate Manager for Lesnes Abbey Woods and works for the London Borough of Bexley.

**Daniel Greenwood**
◆ **London's woodlands**
Daniel worked with volunteers and communities in and around Sydenham Hill Wood from 2012–18, monitoring wildlife populations, improving public access and leading a varied programme of public events. He now lives in West Sussex and works in the South Downs National Park.

**Kabir Kaul**
◆ **Wetlands & reservoirs**
◆ **The future of nature conservation**
Kabir is a young conservationist, wildlife writer and a passionate advocate for London's biodiversity. He is an ambassador for the Cameron Bespolka Trust, RSPB Youth Councillor, London National Park City Ranger and Director of Environment & Conservation for Middlesex Heritage. He has created a popular interactive map, *Nature Reserves of London*, showing every nature reserve and designated wildlife site in the capital. Through blogging, writing, public speaking and social media, he brings focus and awareness to the many green and blue spaces in the capital, what he refers to as the 'Wild Side of London', and how Londoners can make a difference for the wildlife on their doorstep. Kabir has been interviewed by several media outlets including BBC Autumnwatch and *The Observer*, and received the Prime Minister's Points of Light award in March 2020.

**Anna Guerin**
◆ **London's grasslands**
Having worked in education for just over 14 years, Anna decided it was time for a change. Not knowing what to do next, she began volunteering with London Wildlife Trust. Many happy hours of volunteering later and with a new Countryside Management qualification under her belt, Anna now has a full-time position as part of the Brilliant Butterflies team working with local volunteers to restore and create butterfly habitats across South Croydon and Bromley.

# INDEX

**A**corns 114
alpacas 68

**B**adgers 27, 139–40
bats 26, 27–8, 29, 32, 33–5
bee orchids 142–3
bees 15, 39, 49, 57, 98, 114, 184
bumblebees 39, 106, 141
honeybees 91, 106
beetles 26, 27, 35, 39, 57, 77
stag beetles 95, 116–17, 165
violet ground beetle 146
Biggin Wood 164–5
birds 30, 32, 182
bitterns 131
blackbirds 38, 124
blackcaps 60, 138, 139
black redstarts 38
bluebells 160, 161, 167
blue tits 139
bogs 98, 102
Bow Creek Ecology
    Park 51, 52–3
Brent Reservoir 131, 172–3
broom 98, 106–7
brownfields 39, 47
bug hotels 185
bumblebees 106, 141
butterflies 38, 39, 54, 57, 58, 60,
    114, 151, 157, 170, 173
blue 141, 174–5
clouded yellow 169
dingy skipper 141
fritillary 141
hairstreak 68
marbled white 146, 154–5
painted lady 90
buzzards 124, 169, 170, 174

**C**amley Street Natural
    Park 46, 47, 52, 56
caterpillars 60, 68, 142, 146, 154
cattle 59
cattle egret 131
cemeteries 36, 86
Cetti's warbler 124
chaffinches 156
chiffchaffs 138, 139
Colne Valley Regional Park 128
community gardens 70–4
conservation 8–9, 23, 145
future of 180–1
coots 123
cormorants 124
crickets 52–3, 144
crows 39, 81
Culpeper, Nicholas 140

**D**affodils 95, 160, 161
damselflies 49, 57, 173
Dartford warbler 107
Darwin, Charles 102, 150
deer 27, 89
Dexter cattle 59
docklands 38, 46, 47
Dollypers Hill 153
dolphins 12, 17, 19
Downe Bank 152
dragonflies 57, 98, 128, 170, 173
ducks 14, 89, 122–3, 131, 134–5
tufted 14, 122, 172, 173
dunnocks 39

**E**arthworms 27, 89
earwigs 89
eel, European 20–1, 27
elm trees 68

endangered species 20
Epping Forest 36
Estuary Edges 15, 50

**F**ieldfares 123, 125
Finsbury Circus Gardens 81
fish 12, 13, 14, 15, 16, 18, 19, 22
migration 20–1
nocturnal 27
Forest Hill 178
fossils 161
foxes 27, 36, 55, 81, 86, 91, 135, 146
froghopper bugs 146
frogs 27, 54, 63, 64, 65, 128, 162
fungi 89, 110, 112–13, 161

**G**alls 114
geese 122, 123
Gillespie Park 55
glow-worms 26, 27, 147
goats 89
goldfinches 59, 124–5, 139, 156
gorse 98, 106–7
grasshoppers 58, 144
grass snakes 90
grebes 124, 131, 173
Green Chain Walk 110
Greenwich Peninsula Ecology
    Park 48–9, 50, 52
gulls 39, 123–4
Gunnersbury Triangle 162–3
Gutterridge Wood 166

**H**ackney City Farm 66–7
Hampstead Heath 90, 99
hawk moths 146, 147
hazelnuts 114
heather 98, 102–3

heaths 36, 90
hedgehogs 27, 28, 32, 76–7, 90
herbs 184
herons 95, 124, 131, 173
honeysuckle 184
hornbeam 110, 113
house martins 124
hoverflies 39, 54, 57, 140–1, 157
Hutchinson's Bank 151, 174–5

Irises 178, 183
Islington Ecology Centre 55

Jays 114
jellyfish 16
Jubilee Walkway 46

Keston Bog 102
kestrels 90, 145, 147, 169, 170, 174
Kew Gardens 86, 95
kidney vetch 141, 174
kingfishers 14, 53, 90, 132–3
knapweed 141, 155, 156–7
knotweed 38, 54

Lacewings 27, 29
ladybirds 90
lady's bedstraw 139, 140
Lee Valley Regional Park 131
Lesnes Abbey Wood 99, 160–1
Lesnes Heath 98–100, 101, 102
lichens 161
light pollution 28–30, 31
lime trees 173
linnets 38
lizards 102, 128, 144, 145

Mallards 122, 123
marjoram 143
marshes 126
mice 37, 40–1
midges 29, 35
Mile End Ecology Park 57
molluscs 22–3, 27
moorhens 58, 123
mosquitos 91
moths 27, 29, 35, 39, 114, 146
Mudchute Park and Farm 59
mulberry trees 91
mushrooms 110, 112, 113

New Cross Gate Cutting 178
nocturnal wildlife 26–35
noise 32
Northala Fields 85

Oaks 100–1, 114
orchids 142–3, 178
owls 27, 86, 90, 95, 170

Parakeets 86, 88–9, 91
Phoenix Garden 63
pied wagtails 39, 125
pigeons 36, 37, 88, 125
plovers 124
pochards 122
pollution 133, 135
ponds 36, 64, 183
porpoises 12, 17, 19
power stations 82–3
Putney Heath 105, 106

Queen Elizabeth Olympic
    Park 53, 84, 93, 131

Railway Fields 54
Rainham Marshes 126, 128
rats 36, 37, 41, 91
red kites 169
redpolls 125
redwings 90, 125, 139
reed warblers 124, 170, 171
reservoirs 36, 122–35
rewilding 47, 87, 180
Riddlesdown Common 152
robins 30, 39, 90, 124
rooks 81
Roundshaw Downs 153
Ruislip Woods 36
Ruskin, John 94

Saltmarshes 16, 128
sand martins 53
sandpipers 124
seals 12, 17–19
sedge warblers 170, 171
sheep 59, 145, 151
shellfish 12, 14, 16
shoveler ducks 122
shrews 146
silverfish 27
skylarks 139, 145
slowworms 145, 162
snails 22–3
snakes 90, 91
South London Botanical
    Institute Garden 64–5
sparrowhawks 162, 163, 169, 170
sparrows 37, 38, 88, 89
spiders 27, 91, 143
squirrels 88, 91, 114
Stanmore Country Park 169
starlings 59

# INDEX

Sutton Ecology Centre 58
swallows 90, 124
swans 122
swifts 90, 124

**T**amworth pigs 67
teal 53, 134–5
Ten Acre Wood 166–7
terns 49
thistles 141, 155
thrushes 139, 184
toads 32, 60, 61, 162
Tower Hamlets Cemetery Park 57
tufted ducks 14, 122, 172, 173

**V**auxhall City Farm 68–9
Victoria Park 81, 82
voles 15, 91, 145, 177

**W**althamstow Marshes 176–7
warblers 107, 124, 131, 138, 170, 171, 184
wasps 91, 114, 115, 116
wasp spiders 143
wastelands 38–9, 47
weeds 38, 64, 65
weevils 91
wild garlic 160
wildlife gardening 60–1
William Curtis Ecological Park 46, 47, 52
Woodberry Wetlands 54, 55
Wood Farm 169
woodlice 89
woodpeckers 58, 118–19, 142, 162
wrens 39, 58, 89
WWT London Wetland Centre 131

**Y**ellow-rattle 144

# REFERENCES & RESOURCES

**SPECIES PROFILE: HOW TO HELP HEDGEHOGS**
Hedgehog Street
https://www.hedgehogstreet.org
British Hedgehog Preservation Society
https://www.britishhedgehogs.org.uk
email: info@britishhedgehogs.org.uk

**THE GLORY OF PARKS: WHERE NATURE RULES**
The Economics of Biodiversity: The
Dasgupta Review, HM Treasury,
2 February 2021.
Metal, Penny, Insectinside: Life in
the Bushes of a Small Peckham Park,
published by author. Available from
https://insectinside.me
GoParksLondon
https://www.goparks.london

**LONDON'S HEATHLANDS: A UNIQUE LANDSCAPE**
'Lowland heathland a cultural and
endangered landscape', English Nature, 2002.
'Heathland Conservation in London',
London Biodiversity Partnership, 2006.
E Eaton, G Caudullo, S Oliveira, D de Rigo.,
'Quercus robur and Quercus petraea in
Europe: distribution, habitat, usage and
threats', in San-Miguel-Ayanz, J, de Rigo,
D, Caudullo, G, Houston Durrant, T, Mauri,
A (Eds), European Atlas of Forest Tree
Species, Publ. Off. Eu, Luxembourg, 2016.

# PICTURE CREDITS

# ACKNOWLEDGEMENTS

London Wildlife Trust wouldn't be able
to do what we do without our members,
volunteers, supporters and funders.
Our thanks go to all those who helped
make this book possible and who help
make sure that nature can thrive across
London, now and in the future.